GW01607942

Peter Devlin

Fights for Survival

Frederick Muller books by Paul Buddee include:

AIR STORIES
Air Patrol and the Hijackers
Air Patrol and the Saboteurs
Air Patrol and the Secret Intruders
Air Patrol and the Underwater Spies

PONY CLUB STORIES
Ann Rankin and the Boy Who Painted Horses
Ann Rankin and the House on Coolabah Hill
Ann Rankin and the Lost Valley
Ann Rankin and the Great Flood

OUTBACK STORIES
Peter Devlin Fights for Survival
Peter Devlin—Range Rider
Peter Devlin—Buffalo Hunter
Peter Devlin and the Road Bandits

Other Titles:

Osca and Olga
Rupert and Rita
Rattigan Rat
The Unwilling Adventurers
The Mystery of Moma Island
The Escape of the Fenians
The Escape of John O'Reilly
Stand To and Other War Poems

Peter Devlin

Fights for Survival

PAUL BUDDEE

FREDERICK MULLER
LONDON

First published in Great Britain in 1973
by Frederick Muller Ltd., London
Copyright © 1973 Paul Buddee
ISBN 0 584 96989 9

All Rights Reserved. No part of this publication may be reproduced, stored in retrieval system, or transmitted, in any form or by any means, electronic, mechanical, photocopying, recording or otherwise, without the prior permission of Frederick Muller Ltd.

Contents

1 Peter is Down—but Not Out 11
2 A Long Journey is Undertaken 20
3 An Awkward Situation 32
4 A Question of Survival 41
5 A Friend in Need 53
6 The Trip to Boolgana 58
7 Operation Hygiene 71
8 Peter Talks with a Man 81
9 Joe Turns Up 88
10 Cyclone 95
11 Joe to the Rescue 106
12 Good-bye Joe 118
13 Horses do not have Wings—but One Flies 124
14 Escape 131
15 Fortune Shines 147
16 All Thanks to Joe 153
17 All's Right with the World 165

I am deeply grateful to many people who provided background material for the Peter Devlin series. Mr and Mrs Les Schubert and family of Yallalong made it possible for me to gain first-hand information in regard to the running of a modern station. Mr E. A. Wright of Hancock and Wright opened the way for me to explore the great areas in which he and his remarkable partner have been involved. Mr Ken McCamey, the partners' area manager, gave me much of the bushcraft information for this series. Mr Colin Bielski, liaison officer of Hamersley Iron Pty Ltd, supplied me with much on-the-spot material at Mount Tom Price. My old friend, Stuart Buchan, provided me with much unusual material for this series.

The Westralian Flight School gave me valuable assistance in producing the *Air Patrol* series, and again in this series I am indebted to a staff member, Mr Greg Martin, for flight data. Mr A. D. Sieber of the Nature Advisory Service of the W.A. Education Department was also of great assistance in giving information regarding survival in the desert.

To my wife and Mrs D. V. Bremner I wish to pay tribute for their revision of all that I have written in this series, as well as in the *Air Patrol* and the *Ann Rankin* books.

All names, characters, places, and events in this story are entirely fictitious.

Chapter One

PETER IS DOWN—BUT NOT OUT

PETER DEVLIN LAY ON HIS BACK on his bed and looked up at the ceiling. The light reflected through the window made grotesque patterns which wavered and danced before his eyes. From outside, the steady roar of the city traffic dinned in his ears. Now and again the heavy rumble of a large vehicle set the things on his dressing-table jingling and, on occasions, even made his bed shake.

He had done his daily round of the streets. His feet were sore from walking the hard pavements. Indeed, one more day and he would be walking in bare feet, with the remnants of his shoes hanging round his ankles.

"It's the recession," they said. "Look, son, we're putting men off. Sorry."

"Like blooming blazes they were," he reflected. "Likely as not they went home to a hot meal at night and a decent home." He surveyed his own surroundings—the dingy walls, the unwashed window, the bare floor, and the sparse furniture of a small room in a slum area.

"If Mother could only see me now," he reflected. But then on second thoughts he wondered if she would have cared anyway.

The last six months had been hard ones for her in more ways than one.

THE MINISTER OF THE ARMY REGRETS TO ANNOUNCE THAT YOUR HUSBAND, CAPTAIN THOMAS DEVLIN, IS MISSING AFTER A PATROL HE WAS LEADING WAS AMBUSHED IN THE PROVINCE OF TIET DEN CHO.

Since the arrival of that telegram, the days had lengthened into weeks and the weeks into months, and they had learnt nothing further.

Then suddenly, one day, without warning, his mother had gone—just like that. She had left a note.

Goodbye, Peter. I can't take it any longer. Do what you can for yourself.

He had tried. It was little enough. He had watched the new household furniture, which his mother had been buying on time-payment, go piece by piece as the payments became due. Finally, feeling that even he himself might be reclaimed, he had packed his few possessions and moved into a room in a cheap boarding-house the day the next week's rent became due on the flat.

"Let someone else sort it out," he decided. "It's beyond me."

Fortunately his school fees had been paid until the end of the third term. During all this time he had attended school daily, feeling that one thing he must save from the wreck was his educational standing—at least as far as he had taken it.

In this he was successful, as he had gained a pass with credit in his last school examinations. How he would manage to keep going for the two or three years needed for his matriculation, he had no way of knowing.

Peter knew he had been lying there thinking too long. If he dallied any longer, he would go to bed hungry. Not that he had done this very often. He had a plan which had stood him in good stead for some time, though by now he might be overworking it a little.

He had made a careful list of his old school friends. By calling on them at about four o'clock, he was always sure of afternoon-tea, and if he remained long enough, sometimes he was even invited to stay for the evening meal.

In this he imagined himself to be very clever—and perhaps he was—but in most cases, though he did not know it, the mothers were fully informed of his circumstances. It was these who pressed on him the remnants of a pie, some fruit, or a can of something or other, jokingly remarking that such a tall and healthy boy would doubtless enjoy them on the way home.

Today he had the home of Ian Sloan on his list. Mrs Sloan was a large, comfortable person, and he was very fond of her. Ian was away at swimming practice when Peter arrived, but Mrs Sloan, who was fully aware of the situation, invited Peter to join her in a large afternoon-tea. She was trying to reduce her own ample figure, but for the good of the cause endured a second afternoon-tea, in order to ensure that the boy had what she was sure would be his first good meal of the day.

"Of course you'll stay for tea," she said casually enough to deceive Peter. "Ian won't be home till six and you know he'd hate to miss you."

There was nothing casual about her, however, when in the kitchen Peter was helping dry up the cups and saucers. She turned to the boy.

"Why don't you try the country, Peter?"

"What do you mean?"

"Do you want me to spell it out?" She paused. "I've got an uncle—an odd old stick who runs a cattle station, 1200 kilometres out. I'm sure you could be found something there."

"Something might turn up here."

Mrs Sloan glanced at the boy's shoes and clothes. "It would have to be pretty soon, wouldn't it?"

Peter blushed.

"You know?" he asked.

"Let's not get personal, Peter. If I thought it would help, you could come here with Ian, but I think you're a bit too proud."

"I've got to work things out for myself, Mrs Sloan, but I think you might have an idea. I reckon I could make a go of it in the country, while things sorted themselves out. I might even get some time off to continue my studies."

"You'd like me to write to old Uncle Josh?"

"Well, even bed and board wouldn't be something to sneeze at. My finances—" He stopped, embarrassed.

"Okay, Peter. I'll get a letter off tonight. Now forget about it. Go up to Ian's room and amuse yourself with his records until he comes in."

Late that night Peter left the warmth of the Sloan home, with a good supper under his belt and a pair of Ian's shoes on his feet.

"Let's not pretend for once, Peter. Put these shoes on or you'll be in bare feet. In the summer it can be painful on the hot pavements."

Just before he left, Mrs Sloan handed him a letter. "Drop it in the box as you go by," she suggested.

Under a lamp-post Peter studied the address:

Mr Josiah McMichael,
Boolgana Downs,
via Mugee Minder.

He kissed the letter goodbye, as he dropped it

through the slot of the letter-box, and wished it well. He knew that he had enough money to pay the rent for his room for the next three weeks, with little enough left for food or anything else. Where he would find the money for the long trip, he had no idea.

After two weeks had passed without any news, he felt that Mrs Sloan's letter could not have been well received by her relative. Things were now becoming desperate, and he began to sell a number of small articles he had, in order to be able to pay a further week's rent. Beyond that he could not see.

A little good fortune, when he managed to assist the local milkman on a number of occasions, brought him in a few dollars. These he hid carefully under his mattress.

In the middle of the third week he again visited Ian. To his surprise Mrs Sloan produced a letter. It was an ill-written scrawl, and not enough postage had been put on the envelope. It was brief.

Dear Meg,

Send the kid up. He can work for his keep. This ain't no palis but it is beter than the dole.

Josh

"I said he was a strange fellow," said Mrs Sloan, "but it will be a good experience for you.

If you don't like it, you can always come back."

"How do I get there?" the boy asked. "It's going to be pretty expensive."

"Leave that to me," said Mrs Sloan. "We'll call it a loan, to be repaid later. When would you want to leave?"

"Tomorrow," said Peter, thinking of the rent he would have to pay the day after, and now would save. "Is that too soon?"

"We'll soon find out," replied Mrs Sloan, reaching for the telephone.

"You're in luck," she announced a few minutes later. "I've got you the last seat on a tourist charter bus that leaves early tomorrow morning. You're doubly lucky, as you'll get overnight accommodation and meals along the way. They don't often have spare seats on these buses, but it'll save you waiting for the regular weekly bus, which leaves a few days later. The bus will deviate to pass his property; it's some distance off the main road."

She reached for the telephone again. "I'd better send a telegram to Josh to let him know you're coming."

Thus it was that the Sloan family spent the rest of the evening getting Peter under way. A quick search of the family closets revealed a small, sturdy suitcase.

"It's an old one, Peter, and we don't want it back," said Mrs Sloan. "There's a small hole in the bottom edge, but I've put a sheet of plastic lining in to keep out the dust."

She then proceeded to fill it with many of what she called Ian's old things. She also included a torch.

"You may find this handy at night," she explained, "with snakes and things, in those parts."

A large cardboard box was found and filled with as much food as it would hold. Then, with the family calling out its good wishes, Peter was sent on his way.

Mrs Sloan longed to give him a motherly hug and a kiss, but she did not dare. Peter, full of dignity, stood at the door, his arms fully laden, and thanked them gravely for their kindness. He promised immediate repayment of the loan from his first pay.

Mr Sloan wanted to drive the boy back to his lodgings.

"No," Mrs Sloan whispered, "let him go. One day he may break down, but it mustn't be now. He'll be so busy lugging all that stuff back to his room that he'll have no time for sentiment."

Back at his lodgings, the boy found that the rest of his possessions fitted into a large haversack, which he intended to carry on his back. He turned back his bed to recover his small savings. They were gone.

For a moment he sat dazed, and then burst

into tears. Except for some loose silver he had kept in his pocket, he had no money whatsoever. Mrs Sloan's box of goodies would have to last him a long time.

Rising to his feet, he gulped back the tears. "I'm not going to give in to things now," he muttered to himself stubbornly. "Worse things have happened to me."

He counted his resources—less than a dollar in silver in his pockets, a suitcase full of clothes that were good enough for where he was going, a box full of food, and a few treasures in a haversack.

"Maybe I'm richer than I thought," he mused. "At least I have a job to go to."

With that he went to bed for the night, making sure to set his most treasured possession, a travel clock, to ring at five o'clock the next morning.

Chapter Two

A LONG JOURNEY IS UNDERTAKEN

THE SMALL ALARM CLOCK DID NOT let him down. Peter was awakened at the time he had set it.

He was tempted to open the box of food but, realising that it might have to last him over the next few days, he resisted the temptation.

He had a quick shower and slipped into his clothes. As everything had been packed the night before, he had nothing more to do than pick up his luggage and leave.

By nature a courteous boy, he wrote a brief note and left it on the mantelpiece. In it he informed the landlady that he would not be requiring the room any longer. He was not sure that, in lieu of a week's notice, he might not have owed a week's rent. However, as he had paid each week's rent in advance, he did not feel the landlady was losing anything. In any case, there was nothing he could do about it.

It was now first light, but the city streets were deserted. The bus terminal was a long way from his lodgings, but though he was not a big boy, he was strong and wiry enough to manage the load.

Actually, Peter might well have been described as a fine-looking boy. He was not yet fully developed, but was still tall for his age. He had a long nose, brown eyes, and an oval, clean-cut face, surmounted by a mass of unruly but well-kept brown hair.

He had a good skin, sun-bronzed through much swimming and surfing, and quite well-proportioned limbs. In movement he was quick and decisive. At school he had been more than average in athletics and sport. Physically, he was still more boy than man. Beneath it all he had a very keen mind, sensitive to the things about him, but strong enough to stand up to the realities of life.

As he walked to the depot, he wondered if he was running away from things. He comforted himself with the thought that he could consider it a matter of sheer survival rather than just of flight.

The huge coach was standing ready to go when he arrived, although the call to board had not yet been given.

He entered the terminal and reported at the travel counter. When he received his ticket he was pleased to notice that coupons for meals along the way were attached. He handed in his suitcase and haversack, and from a rack picked up a map of the area which showed in detail the roads, rivers, towns, and stations they would pass. He then moved over to a row of seats in the waiting-room.

With the bonus of meals along the way, there was no reason why he should not take his breakfast from the box of food. He untied the string and opened it. On the top of the food was an envelope with some writing on it.

Please excuse us Peter—just a bit more to pay back. You may need it.

Inside was a ten-dollar bill and some silver. The boy felt his eyes moisten, but suddenly he felt the day brighten, and the memory of the loss of his small savings of the night before did not now seem so bitter.

He delved into the box with gusto, making sure that the money was safely inside his shirt pocket. To make doubly sure he would not lose it, he found a safety pin and, putting it through the shirt and the money, made it secure. Somehow he did not seem so alone now.

The huge terminal was gleaming from the efforts of the cleaners during the previous night. The well-polished floors awaited the onslaught of the thousands of feet which would pass over them during the day. The boy pushed back into the softness of the padded seat he was sitting on, enjoying the feeling of luxury around him.

It was a world he had once known, and this return to it, if even for a brief period, was a welcome respite. Near him, someone had discarded the daily paper. He slid along the seat and recovered it, glancing at the headlines, but reserving the pleasure of reading it closely at his leisure later in the day.

Outside the sun had already come up. It would be a hot summer's day, he knew, but this would not worry him in the air-conditioned coach. Not that he found travel a discomfort. He was agog to get going, and to watch the panorama of the country unfold before him.

His travels in the past had been confined to the coastal regions and wheat farms nearer the city, and he had no idea, except from what he had read, of what lay before him.

He had no idea either of what would be required of him on the station. He could ride a horse quite well—horse-riding had been one of his father's pleasures. He could drive a car or a truck, and had done so on the wheat farm his Uncle Ted owned, but of course it would be a year or so before he could obtain a licence to drive on the highways. He reflected that he might have been able to get a job on his uncle's farm, were it not for the fact that his uncle had now retired and was in the process of selling his property.

He had heard that the cattle stations still

used horses, but on the big sheep holdings they now used motor bikes and aeroplanes to round up the stock. He wondered what he would find at Boolgana Downs.

"Will all passengers for Route 237 please take their seats! Your coach leaves in five minutes exactly."

The disembodied voice from the loudspeakers brought him back to reality.

He made a quick dash to the toilet, more for the pleasure of enjoying the luxury of the hot and cold water in the basins, with the liquid soap and the paper towels, than because he needed to go. He wiped his face over with a towel, dried his hands, and went through the swing doors to the ramp where his coach was waiting.

It was surrounded by a crowd of people. Men were loading the last of the luggage and the goods in the huge compartment at the rear and the smaller compartments underneath. The milling crowd seemed to surge back and forth, people saying their goodbyes, or trying in dumb show to make last-minute conversation with those already in the bus and imprisoned behind the thick glass windows, sealed shut on account of the air-conditioning.

Peter stood watching and enjoying the scene, until suddenly the great diesel motor roared into life and the driver, recognising him as a passenger, nodded his head in warning. Clutching his cardboard box the boy swung aboard and the pneumatic door hissed shut behind him.

To his delight he found that he had a single seat, right in the front, just behind the driver, allowing him a good view of the road ahead. He also had a side window all to himself. Looking back at the pantomime of the last-minute exchanges between the passengers inside, and those who had come to see them off, outside, Peter smiled. He placed his box in the luggage rack and settled down in his seat to await in luxurious comfort the moment of departure.

It was not long in coming. Slowly the heavy coach gathered speed as it swung out of the depot. Then they were out in the traffic of the busy city, now getting ready for another day.

From his vantage point, the boy was able to admire the deftness with which the driver manipulated his huge vehicle with its forty passengers. In and out of the mass of vehicles on the road they manoeuvred, round through side streets to avoid busy intersections, along congested subways with the trains roaring across above their heads, through the sprawling suburbs and their shopping centres, until suddenly it all seemed to drop away, and the vehicle was travelling down an expressway at eighty kilometres an hour, as if anxious to move ahead on the journey. Peter watched the world slide by like a kaleidoscope of vivid impressions.

The sun had now risen on the side of the coach where Peter was sitting, but already the air-conditioning was hissing and blowing to provide for the comfort of the passengers. Peter reached up and twiddled the knobs above his head, resting his head back on the seat. Here was something worth enjoying, even if only for a short time. He was determined to make the most of every minute of it.

Outside, the suburbs were gradually giving way to an occasional field or two. The country was brown and dry, but it had a beauty which delighted him. There was still plenty of water about, and the cattle in the fields seemed contented enough. Soon these were left behind on the plains below, as the road began to climb through the hills.

At a large town, ninety kilometres from the city, the coach stopped briefly. It gave those on board a short while to go outside, stretch their legs, and snatch a quick can of drink if they so desired. Before the end of the journey, the coach would have clocked up another 2000 kilometres. Peering into the driver's compartment, Peter noticed that it had already travelled 135 785 kilometres.

When the vehicle started again, Peter took a pencil and did some calculations. Figures always delighted him.

"Phew," he muttered to himself. "If this crate were to do a hundred kilometres an hour, twenty-four hours a day, it would take it four hundred and seventeen days to travel a million kilometres non-stop." He was sorry there was no one sitting alongside him, with whom he could share his discovery.

He looked over his shoulder at the seat behind, but he saw sitting there an old lady, who had dozed off to sleep. The man alongside her had his nose deep in a book. Peter shrugged his shoulders and turned his attention to the road again.

The forested hill country had now given way to a plain of wheat lands where large flocks of sheep nibbled away at the stubble from the previous season's crop.

At midday, the coach stopped for forty-five minutes for lunch. Coming from the coolness of the air-conditioning, Peter felt the outside air hit his face like the heat from a blast-furnace.

"Reckon it will be in the forties today," the driver remarked. "It will get hotter as we go further north."

Armed with his food coupon, Peter entered the large dining-room of the roadhouse. Everything gleamed with cleanliness. Here again the air-conditioning was in full blast, keeping out both the heat and the dust.

The boy was hungry, and he decided to make up for what he had been missing over the past few months by ordering a large T-bone steak, eggs, tomatoes, and chips. When he followed the steak with a cassata and two cups of coffee, and finished all the bread and butter on the table, the old lady at the same table said, "Dear, dear, what a healthy appetite. You look as though you haven't had a good meal for a month."

"Not too many, ma'am, but this certainly makes up for it." He left the table regretfully.

He was sitting in his seat waiting for the bus to resume its journey, when he felt a hand tapping his head. It was the old lady behind him.

"Take these, dear," she said, handing over two large packets of chocolate. "It will keep the worms from biting until tea."

Peter thanked her but resisted the temptation to tear off the wrappers. Instead, he put the kind gift in the cardboard box Mrs Sloan had given him.

During the morning he had eaten the sandwiches she had cut. Sensibly, she had filled the rest of the box with packets of biscuits, some small tins of meat-loaf, and two cans of soft drink. Not sure of what he would meet at his journey's end, he wanted to keep some food as a standby.

The coach was now roaring along at a speed of over eighty kilometres an hour. By the middle of the afternoon it had passed beyond the edge of the wheat lands, which suddenly dropped behind. In their place the low mulga had taken over.

Peter had imagined it was the custom of these great overlander buses to keep going all night. However, early that evening as they were passing through a town they pulled into a large motel parking area.

"We start again at six ack emma sharp tomorrow, folk," the driver called as he left his seat.

He and his relief driver moved from the bus.

"Come and have tea with us, youngster," one of them said to Peter. "You looked lonely sitting by yourself all day."

One looked at his notes. "See we drop you off at the Boolgana Downs turnoff," he remarked. "They expecting you?"

"I hope so," said Peter. "Is it far to the station?"

"Oh, forty or fifty kilometres, but it's too far to walk on a hot day." They both laughed.

"You a friend of old McMichael?"

"No. I'm just going there to work. Couldn't get any in the city."

"You'll get work there all right."

"What do you mean?"

"Let's get something to eat," said the other driver, deliberately changing the subject.

After the meal Peter was shown his accommodation in the motel. An air-conditioner was in full operation at one end of his room. A door opened on to a shower and toilet area. The boy stripped off his clothes and enjoyed the powerful spray of water. This seemed to take away the aches which had developed in his body from a day of sitting in the one position.

He wrapped a towel round himself and moved back to the bedroom. Opposite him was a small refrigerator, and in it a large jug of iced water. He took his cans of drink from the haversack and put them in the refrigerator.

On a table by his bed was a tray with a hot-water jug, cups, and packages of milk powder, sugar, and instant tea and coffee. This was luxury he had never dreamed of, and he made himself two cups of coffee immediately. It seemed impossible that the city was now nearly 800 kilometres away.

He opened the outer door, but the hot blast from outside and a cloud of insects forced him to close it again. That it was expected the insects would invade was made clear when he found a can of spray on the table. He sprayed liberally and watched the host around the light-globe fall and gradually die.

He had been too busy watching the changing

scenery on the trip to read his newspaper. With the inducement of a handy lamp at the head of his bed, he now opened it and read until he found his eyes closing with tiredness.

His last thoughts were of pleasantness in his present surroundings and happiness at the events of the day. Tomorrow could look after itself.

Chapter Three

AN AWKWARD SITUATION

PETER'S DREAMWORLD CAME suddenly to an end after some five hours of travelling the next day.

The coach came to a stop in the middle of nowhere. The driver pointed to him and to a rough weatherbeaten sign on the side of the road.

BOOLGANA DOWNS 43 KILOMETRES

The relief driver went to the luggage compartment and got out his case and haversack.

"Good luck, kid. Doesn't look as if anyone is here to meet you. Hope someone comes soon."

Peter lugged the load to the side of the road and the coach roared off in a cloud of dust. He was standing alone under the hot midday sun, shocked at the sudden change in his condition, though he knew he should have expected it.

As far as he could see, there stretched the flat country, with saltbush and spinifex as its only covering. In moving off the road, he trod on one of the bushes and the sharp spines penetrated his trousers and broke off in his legs. He cursed and, pulling up his trouser legs, picked out the larger pieces. He could still feel the smaller points which he could not pull out.

Peter was not in the habit of wearing a hat, and did not have one on his head when he moved from the coach. He opened his case and took out a towel, which he placed over his head like an Arab head-dress.

The ancient sign pointed down a rough and winding track. He was surprised to find that the sign showed the changeover from miles to kilometres, but on closer inspection he found that the word "miles" had been whitewashed over and "kilometres" substituted, while the actual figures had remained unchanged.

He looked into the distance, hoping that he might see the dust of an approaching vehicle coming down the track but, except for a willy-willy or two in the distance, there was nothing to break the monotony of the hot, bare countryside.

A kilometre away, he could see another track, which apparently also branched in from the main road. There was a forty-gallon drum lying on its side, acting as a primitive mail-box, or holder for stores left for the station.

He moved over to it, taking his luggage. There was a bundle of letters inside and, prominently on top of them, a telegram addressed to Josiah McMichael. Struck by a sudden suspicion, he extracted the telegram and opened it. It was the one Mrs Sloan had promised to send, announcing his arrival.

Peter knew that he was in a serious situation. He had already noticed that traffic on the road was sparse. Here he was, stranded, in the middle of nowhere, and likely to remain so for some time, unless someone came out from the station to collect the mail.

He knew now that it was useless for him to wait. No one knew he was there. Forty-three miles or forty-three kilometres—call them what you would—were too many for him to travel safely in the heat, with a box of biscuits, a tin or two of meat, and two cans of soft drink.

Peter knew that most stations were located on watercourses and rivers. He took out his map of the bus route, to study the situation, waving his hands wildly to keep his face free of the flies which had attached themselves to him the moment he had left the coach.

Just before leaving his motel, he had scooped up all the remaining tea and coffee packages, with the sugar and dried milk and, as a final gesture, had taken the insect repellent and put it in his food-box. He took the can out and sprayed round his face. The insects fell away.

A close study of the map showed him two things. One was that, to reach his setting-down point, the coach had deviated along a loop road off the main road, and the main highway was actually some twenty kilometres away across country. Unless a vehicle was to come specially to Boolgana Downs or the next station some forty kilometres further on, he could not expect any traffic. The second thing he noticed was that about four kilometres along, the road was cut by what was designated the Dankin River.

It was probably dry, as all the other rivers, creeks, and streams had been over the last few hundred kilometres, but he knew that sometimes one could obtain seepage water by digging.

In case someone came out from the station to recover the mail, he tore a sheet from a notebook in his haversack and left a message attached to the mail.

I have gone down to wait at the Dankin River. Will leave my luggage here.

Peter Devlin

There was no point in carrying all his gear with him. He put his jacket in the haversack, and then hid the suitcase and haversack under some bushes on the side of the road. With his food-box containing his two tins of drink under his arm he set off down the road.

He knew that, with his scant supply of water, it would be almost impossible to get back to the main highway. The long walk across country would provide him with even less chance of being found than if he stayed on the road he was on.

"This is ridiculous," he muttered to himself, hardly able to believe that, in such a short period of time, his condition had changed from the security of being a passenger in a comfortable air-conditioned motor coach, to being a lone figure in a parched countryside, with no one aware of his predicament.

He had one thing in his favour. He was still fresh, and his immediate objective, the Dankin River, was not more than an hour's walk away. He was glad he had the towel, as he had no wish to add sun-stroke to his misfortunes.

After he had been walking about fifty minutes, he was sure that he could see, some distance away, some sort of vegetation that was not saltbush. A few moments later, he saw that he was coming to a low line of greenery.

He had reached it almost before he realised the fact. The road took a sudden deep dip, and he saw that what he had imagined to be small bushes were the tops of some quite large trees, growing in a deep depression, which was apparently the watercourse. They were either coolabahs or river gums. He was not expert enough to decide, but they would be a source of shade. As they appeared to be growing strongly, the dry river-bed might not be as dry underneath as it appeared.

He ran down the depression, and on to the low-level concrete crossing for the road. Fifty metres away, a number of dead sheep lay rotting in the sun and he could smell their sickly odour. He jumped off the crossing and walked upstream from them—at least it would have been upstream if the water had been running. The trees were growing thickly and provided a welcome shade. He sat down not too far from the crossing, glad to remove the towel from his head.

"What next?" he asked himself. He had no answer.

He moved his tongue over his dry lips and remembered his precarious water situation. He might not have an answer as to what he had to do in general, but he knew that there was something he must attend to in particular—the finding of some water, as soon as he could.

When he had rested, he found a branch of a tree and began to dig in the coarse, red sand of the river-bed. Under the dry surface, he found the soil was moist, but though he dug down deeply, no seepage appeared.

It was inviting to sit in the shade of the trees, but he felt that he should walk up the river-bed, in the hope of finding an area where some water could be found under the surface. He was so intent upon studying the whole width of the river that, before he knew it, he was some half a kilometre up the river and could barely see the crossing.

For some little time he had heard a dull sound in his ears without realising what it was, and when realisation struck him, it was too late. The sound increased to a roar. A large truck tore over the crossing, and with a swish climbed the other side and disappeared in a cloud of dust.

Peter ran back to the track, as if by doing so he could in some magical way stop the truck, but by the time he arrived it had gone from sight and sound.

Cursing himself for being a fool for not doing so before, he piled a cairn of stones in the middle of the crossing, so that nothing else could pass without stopping.

These exertions had put the final seal on his thirst, and he took one of his precious cans of drink from his box. He noticed that it did not have a pull-top. He felt in his pocket for his opener, and then realised that he had left it in the pocket of his jacket which he had packed in his haversack.

He looked round until he found a sharp-pointed stone. Then, taking another larger stone, he put the can on the concrete of the crossing, placed the point of the sharp stone on the lid, and then hit it with the larger stone.

The can was hot, and as the point of the stone cut into its top, it squirted its contents all over him. He had to try and catch as much as he could before it all blew out. His face and hands were sticky with the drink, and the flies, realising that here was an unexpected treat, fell on him in delighted swarms.

He had been too vigorous in his attempts at opening, and the can was leaking down the seam. There was no other course than to drink it all.

His immediate thirst was quenched. With this feeling of satisfaction, he weakened in his resolve to move up the river again in search of water, making as his excuse the possibility that perhaps another vehicle might come, and he needed to be close. Instead he lay down in the shade, pulling the towel over his head to keep off the flies, and was soon asleep.

This did not mean that Peter was not anxious about his present situation. He was, but this was quite different in his mind from being alarmed about it. At fifteen, one has a rugged optimism that under all circumstances something will turn up.

The coach that had brought him to the area moved off the highway only on the rare occasions when it had to drop passengers at the two stations. The supply- and mail-truck went through only once a week. It had apparently passed on its outward run the day before, and he had just missed it on its return trip, when he had been looking for water up river.

Though he did not know it, his only chance of survival lay in the decisions he would make when he awoke.

Chapter Four

A QUESTION OF SURVIVAL

WHEN PETER AWOKE, the sun had gone down. In half an hour it would be dark. Obviously nothing had come along the road or it would have awakened him.

To be sure he peered over to the causeway, but his pile of stones was still intact.

For the first time the boy began to feel a slight uneasiness. He took his food-box and looked in it. The sight of the remaining can of drink reminded him that if he wished to get the benefit of its entire contents, he would have to find a more economical way of opening it than with two pieces of stone.

He debated as to whether it was worth the walk back to where he had left his things to get his opener. It would take two hours to get there and back. He found that it was much cooler now the sun had disappeared. This helped him decide. If it became cold during the night, he might need his coat.

An hour later, though by now it was dark, he

had returned to where he had hidden his suitcase and haversack. He had not previously fully examined the contents of the case and he now did so. He remembered one thing—just before she had closed it, Mrs Sloan had slipped in a torch. The boy groped inside the case and found it. The light made things easier.

Most of the things in it would be of no immediate use back at the river-bed, and he had no intention of carrying back the suitcase itself. Just the same, a nagging suspicion that he might have to endure a longer stay than he thought made him decide to take the haversack, removing from it unnecessary articles, which he put in the case.

He discarded his soap and toilet gear, but illogically left in his small travelling alarm clock. He put in some handkerchiefs, some socks and another towel. He transferred from the case a few pairs of underpants, and a spare pair of trousers, but left the singlets. He already had in his haversack a few boxes of matches, a sheath knife, a plastic cup, and the jacket he had discarded earlier in the day. He felt in the pocket to make sure that the can-opener was still in it.

A prickling sensation in his legs made him realise that he had moved back over some spinifex. He changed his mind and took out two singlets.

"I don't like this stuff," he reflected. "If by any chance I have to walk through it, I might stop the wretched stuff from penetrating if I tie the singlets round my ankles."

He found an envelope between the singlets. Ian had also decided to make his contribution to his welfare. Inside was three dollars.

"Jolly good," he thought ironically. "Just enough to get me a nice taxi down the track. Five hundred dollars would be just as useless to me now."

It was strange to reflect on. A week ago three dollars would have represented a pretty good meal. Now, its most useful function would be to light a fire with.

He had a heap of junk in his haversack which would be of equal use to him—a mouth organ, a small coin collection, and an old camera which he had put in a plastic bag to keep the dust out. He transferred all these things to the suitcase.

Struck by a sudden thought, he removed the plastic bag and put it in his pocket. Mrs Sloan had wrapped up a suit she had given him in a large sheet of plastic. He took this off and put it in his haversack. He felt around for the lining which she had put at the bottom of the case. He pulled the sheet out. It opened out to about half a metre square.

"Could be quite handy if the worst happens,"

he mused. What this meant, he did not pause to consider.

In due course he had all he felt he wanted in his haversack, and he had put all he did not want in the case. He snapped it shut, and pushed it under a bush.

Then, by the light of the torch, he steered his way clear of any spinifex, until he was on the road. It was now dark, but he could feel the road beneath his feet and he snapped off the light.

He arrived back safely at the river and found his original camp. By now he was hungry, and so he decided to open one of the tins of meat from his food-box.

He did so and ate it slowly. It was quite satisfying, but it made him thirsty.

"What do I do now? Have a drink? If I do have a drink, do I drink it all, or save some for tomorrow?" In the end he decided to open the can and have a few sips.

This time he was more careful and, as the opener bit into the top, he had his mouth nearby. Just the same the amount that sprayed up was almost too much for him, and some went up his nose.

It was a lemon drink, and he was surprised to find that even the small amount he had sprayed into his mouth refreshed him. He put a wad of paper in the small hole. There was a sizzling sound for a few minutes, while the gas continued to seep out, but presently this stopped.

There was enough drink left in the can for at least another day. Surely, during this time, someone would come down the road.

Sitting down on the river-bank, he began to wish he was a year or so older, and had been able to go on the safaris which were part of the training of the senior cadets of his school. They had been trained in survival drill in hot country. He remembered listening to their talk about it.

"No one," the head boy had told the juniors, with the superiority of experience, "need ever die of thirst, even if there is no visible water."

"How come?" a sceptic had asked.

"Use a bit of plastic, some green leaves and leave the rest to nature."

This had been cryptic enough to make him want to know more.

"You dig a hole about half a metre deep in a damp area, fill the hole with leaves, then cover it with plastic, and let the sun do the rest."

"What happens?"

"The sun causes the water to condense on the plastic and you catch it in a tin or something."

Seeing the plastic in his case had brought this conversation back to Peter's mind.

"If no one comes, I'll try it out tomorrow,"

he decided and then, wishing he had not dumped his mouth organ, he took the towels and, using them as a pillow, settled down to sleep.

He woke at dawn. Three large red kangaroos bounded slowly past him, going upstream. He sat up, but they took no notice of him. At the top of the bank, two emus stalked by.

"Must be some water around," he decided. "I'll go and have a look, later."

He moved down to the river-bed, deciding to try the new idea of getting water. There was no pressing urgency. Cars or trucks were sure to come down the road during the day.

He scooped out quite a large hole in mid-stream, in a damp spot, took his knife and cut off the most succulent leaves from the river gums and put them in the hole. He put his cup in the middle and, stretching one of the pieces of plastic across the hole, he sealed it on all sides with sand.

He ate a small breakfast of biscuits, and then took one mouthful of the now flat drink and replaced the can in his box.

On a number of occasions during the rest of the morning he moved from the shade to the top of the rise, in order to look back along the road. In each case, the same red track ran into the distance, with nothing on it.

After he had done this a number of times,

Peter realised that he was making himself hot unnecessarily. The feeling of sweat running down his back warned him that it would be unwise to do this again. Somehow he must curb his impatience.

He could see the piece of plastic in the river-bed and early in the afternoon his curiosity overcame him. Putting a towel over his head, he decided to inspect the result.

The result was disappointing. The underside of the plastic was wet, but none of the moisture had dripped into the cup. He sat alongside the hole, wondering how he must direct the water to drop into the cup.

Then he could have kicked himself. The plastic was taut across the hole. It needed to slope down into it like a funnel, the bottom pointing over the cup. For a moment he found himself wondering how to do this, and then he felt foolish when he realised the solution. Near at hand were a number of small stones. He took them and placed enough of them in the middle of the plastic to make it sag. It was, he hoped, right above the cup. Then he sealed the hole.

When by late afternoon nothing had come down the road, Peter really began to feel worried. By now, surely someone should have come out from the station to get the mail. Before it became dark he decided to go up and see.

By the time he arrived at the mail-drum, the sun had gone down. He shone his torch into it. There was another bundle of mail which he had not noticed before, further back inside. He pulled it out to examine the dates and found it was from the drop of the week before.

"The old man isn't very keen to get his mail," he reflected. "Hope it isn't another week before he decides to collect it."

On his return to the river, he decided that he would have to do something drastic about the water.

An inspection of the hole he had dug showed that this time he had had some success, as about a centimetre of water lay in the bottom of the cup.

He tasted it gingerly. It was warm and insipid. He knew that he must have a good drink and took up the remains of the can.

"Here goes," he said to himself. "I either find water, or someone comes, or I'll be pretty thirsty, pretty soon."

He drained the can and was going to throw it away, but decided against it, as another idea occurred to him. He took the opener and removed the lid completely.

As no cars had come in the daytime, it was unlikely any would pass at night, but to make sure, he went to the stones and made an arrow pointing upstream.

Then with the light of his torch, he took up the plastic from the hole, recovered the cup, took the rest of the plastic from his pack, and walked upstream.

About a kilometre along, he found a place where the kangaroos had been scratching in the river-bed. The ground was moister than it was at the place where he had camped. He proceeded a little further. In one place he found that the animals had dug down deeply. A little water was lying in the scratchings. He went on and found a small pool, but the water was so brackish that he spat it out.

However, it gave him an idea. The tiny patch of water was not more than a metre square. He moved a little away from it and scratched out a hole half a metre deep, and as wide as the plastic would allow. He put the cup on a rock at the bottom and then made a small drain to run some of the water from the pool. He put a stone on top of the plastic to make the necessary depression.

A few metres away he dug another hole and put the can in, again on a rock. He ran another drain from the small pool into the hole. By the torch light he watched the water slowly trickle into it. He placed his other piece of plastic in position above it and then returned downstream to the road. There was nothing more he could do.

The next day was the worst of them all. Knowing he had no water made him feel thirstier than he really was. He knew that his very existence depended on whether the two stills would produce water which he could drink. This time he was sensible and though he found it difficult to do so, he lay in the shade all day, moving no more than was necessary.

He did not wait for the sun to go down to return upstream to his stills. In a few minutes he would know if he was to survive. It was hard not to run the last distance when he saw the plastic-covered holes.

The small drains had ceased to run. He tore the plastic away from the first hole, but he was careful not to rip it in his eagerness. The hole had water over the bottom and to his relief he found the cup more than half full. He took the cup and, regardless of the consequences, gulped the contents down.

Almost immediately he felt the benefit. Very carefully he replaced the cup and, judging that there was enough water in the hole for his purpose, replaced the plastic. Then he moved to the other hole.

In this case he was more than surprised. The can was brimming over. He looked over at the pool. It still lay there, though with a little less water in it than the day before.

One thing was sure now, however. He had a

supply of water that would last for some time. He gave a sigh of relief. He cleared the water channel to the second hole and wished that he had another container. He felt his shirt pocket and found another piece of plastic. It was the bag he had used to wrap around his camera.

He examined it carefully. To be sure it was airtight, he blew into it. It showed no sign of a leak.

He took the can, drank a little from the top of it, and poured the rest into the plastic bag. He twisted the top of the bag round his finger, and tied it into a knot. He had a watertight container full of water to last him for the next day.

With new spirit, he replaced the can in the second still and returned to the road. It was now dark, but he was feeling much happier than he had on the upward trip.

He felt hungry again and ate the last tin of meat and half a dozen biscuits. He still had plenty of biscuits and the water in the plastic bag, used carefully, would prevent him getting as thirsty as he had done before.

In any case something *had* to come down the road at some time!

Chapter Five

A FRIEND IN NEED

ANOTHER DAY PASSED. His water supply assured, Peter felt that he could continue for some time, but he knew that his food could not last forever, and that a diet of sweet biscuits was not doing him much good. Already he could feel a weakness in his knees, though he tried to pretend it was not there.

He made his way upstream, well before dusk this time, drank his fill from the store; refilled the plastic bag and then, after resetting the stills, started to walk back. On arrival, Peter looked to the cairn of stones on the road. As he did so he saw a movement at the crossing. He felt that it was either a kangaroo or an emu, but as he approached and the form did not move, with a wild hope he yelled out, "Hi!"

"Hi," came the reply.

With newfound strength, Peter ran along the river-bed towards the crossing.

A musical voice called out, "Hey! What you do here? Hey!"

"I'm in trouble," Peter called out. "Is there anyone with you?"

"No."

"Where do you come from?"

"Back there—" and an arm waved vaguely.

By now they were close. Facing him, on the causeway, was a slim young lad of about thirteen or fourteen, with a mop of wild brown hair, and large brown eyes set in a long face. He was dressed in blue jeans, which did not hide his brown skin.

The boy repeated his initial question.

"What you do here?"

"I'm waiting to be picked up from Boolgana Downs. Got off the bus a few days back. No one came out."

"Hey! You're the city kid, hey!"

"Yes. And pretty hungry too. Got any food?"

"Enough."

"Enough for me?"

"I said enough. That means enough."

"You're a funny kid, but I'm pretty glad to see you. How did you get here?"

"Rode. My horse is back at my camp."

"Where's that?"

"Down there," the boy said, pointing downstream. "There's a bit of water for the horse. He doesn't need much. He's used to it."

"What about you?"

"I find plenty. More than you."

"I'm doing okay. I was able to make a still."

"What's that?"

Peter showed him the bag of water and tried to explain, but he could see the boy was not interested.

"Come on, if you want to eat."

Peter ran back for his haversack and, grabbing it, returned to the causeway. The boy was throwing away the rocks which Peter had placed on it.

"No need for this," he said. "You're with me. You're safe enough."

Peter laughed at the boy's assurance. "I hope so. I wouldn't have lasted much longer. Do many trucks come down the road?"

"Maybe next week."

"Heck! It's a good thing you came when you did. I was starting to get pretty worried."

He followed the boy along the river-bed and, as it was now dark, took out the torch and shone it ahead.

"Put it out. I can't see," said the boy.

Peter did so, hoping that he could follow the boy. Half a kilometre further along, the whinny of a horse told him that they had reached the boy's camp. There was the smell of smoke. On the side of the river-bank Peter could see the light of a small fire. The exciting smell of something stewing came to him.

"Have some dinner," the boy invited.

Peter saw that there was only the billy and no plates. Struck by an idea, he drank the water from the plastic bag.

"Pour some on here," he invited and shone his torch on the plastic.

The boy tipped half the contents on to the plastic which Peter had put on the ground.

Peter did not pause to ask what it was, but ate it with gusto. It was the most delicious meal he had ever had. He licked the plastic clean and then, knowing that this might have to be his plate for some time, put it away in his pocket.

"Thanks. That was wonderful. My name's Peter. What's yours?"

"Jet Mercedes Benz."

"What!"

"Yep. My pa's name is Jacky Windmill. My uncle is named Tom Tomahawk."

Peter did not comment, but Jet was quite happy to explain.

"I'm a bitzer—bit of white, bit of the other. Some of the station folk name us so they can know who they're paying—when they do."

"Don't they?"

"Not ol' McMichael, the —. What do you think I hang round for? Maybe he'll pay one day and then I'll scoot off."

"Bad as that?"

"Worse."

"Say, you're not having me on, are you? What else is wrong?"

"You'll find out."

"What are you doing up here?"

"Ol' Mac's place is about a day's ride away. He made me run down the river to the road to see if I could pick up any stray sheep before the water comes down."

"The water?"

"Yep. Due any time. Big rains in the hills. Might even be safer to get out tonight."

"Didn't see any rain."

"There wasn't any here, but there was plenty in the hills a hundred kilometres away."

"One minute I'm nearly dying of thirst and the next I can be drowned," said Peter. "I wouldn't have known. I've been sleeping in the river-bed every night."

"Some people have all the luck."

"I suppose you could put it that way. Let's get moving then. I've had too much trouble staying alive the last few days to want to end up drowned."

"That would be very funny," said Jet with a giggle.

"Very funny. I'm dying laughing."

Chapter Six

THE TRIP TO BOOLGANA

THEY MOVED THE HORSE and their possessions to a suitable place as near the top of the bank as possible. If they moved from the edge of the deep cutting they would find themselves among the spinifex, and even Jet objected to this.

With a good meal under his belt, and tired from the excitement of the changing fortunes of the day, Peter slept soundly.

He was awakened suddenly by a great roar. It was first light. Jet was already on his feet and moving with the horse right up the bank. Peter grabbed his things and followed.

It was just as well he moved when he did. A great roaring, swirling bank of water was advancing down the river-bed, carrying everything loose in front of it. It had a head of at least six metres, and was swishing even higher along the banks.

In a few seconds the place where they had been sleeping was under the rushing water, and some even spilled over the edges and ran over the countryside. Peter found he was standing in water.

"Should we go further back?" he asked.

"Wouldn't do much good. This is flat country and so if it does flood, it will soon spread. But this is a safe one. It will rush down and then there won't be any sign of it in a day or so."

"You mean it will stop flowing?"

"Sure. The rain hasn't set in for the summer. This is a flash flood. Comes up and goes down pretty fast. It's too bad if you're crossing the river when one comes down. You were lucky I came along."

"What do we do now?"

"Go back downstream to ol' Mac. That is, if the water doesn't get him—hope it does."

Peter looked at the boy.

"He's that mean?"

"Meaner."

Jet had a few tins of food in his saddlebags and they opened one and had breakfast.

"What was in the stew last night, Jet?"

"You wouldn't like it if I told you."

Peter laughed, but decided not to investigate further.

"At least I know what's in a can," he said. "What about something to drink?"

Jet had a large old-fashioned water-bottle which was nearly full. Peter produced his tea, sugar, and milk powder.

"Let's have a brew," he suggested. Jet had cleaned out his billy with sand the night before. They half-filled it and, as by now they were away from the river-bank and the water had failed to follow them, there was enough dry tinder to make a fire.

Jet waved the milk powder away.

"Don't hold with that stuff except in damper. I like mine black and strong."

The sun was up, but not yet hot enough to cause Peter any discomfort. When the water was warm enough, Peter put in the instant tea and, as a concession to Jet, handed him the billy of black tea, liberally laced with sugar. The boy drank half and handed the billy back to Peter, who dropped in the powdered milk.

He was still thirsty enough to feel that the tea was nectar, and he drained it to the last drop.

"Plenty of water now," said Jet, "but it will be a bit muddy and taste of dead sheep."

"I'm still so thirsty that if it tasted of dead elephants, I'd still drink it."

"Haven't heard of any of them around here," said Jet gravely, "but I guess all dead animals taste the same."

"Let's get going," suggested Peter, now not quite so happy about the contents of the previous night's meal.

They travelled all day. At times both used

the horse; at others, one rode and the other walked. The sun was relentless, and Peter used his towel again. Even Jet took out a large floppy hat and put it on.

Jet seemed in no hurry to reach his destination. He searched for any signs of animals.

Early in the afternoon, they came upon a dozen sheep and a little later some cattle. Six of the cows had calves. Jet inspected them.

"The cows don't belong to us but the calves are clean-skins. That won't stop ol' Mac. He's building up a herd from O.P.'s and no one can catch him."

"O.P.'s?"

"Other people's. He won't touch anything with a brand on, but he'll take any clean-skins and put his own brand on them."

"But won't the calves want to stay with their mothers? The cows would have one brand and the calves another."

"Not the way ol' Mac does it. He'll 'sleeper' them."

Peter looked at him with inquiry.

"Oh—you don't understand?"

"No."

"Well, ol' Mac will come up here and nick the tongues of the calves. This makes it hard for them to suck, and so they'll leave their mas and have to eat fodder. A week or so later he'll come up here and drive the calves off. They won't want their mas and their mas won't want them."

"Won't he get caught?"

"He hasn't up till now. It's hard to prove, except from the fact that a lot of cattle round here apparently aren't having as many calves as they used to."

Peter pointed to the sheep in the distance. "I didn't think you mixed sheep and cattle," he said.

"You don't. The sheep eat too close, but if you keep them in separate paddocks, it's all right. The big blokes round here do all right, but Mac just mixes them. He'll go broke in time and then one of the big fellows will take over and make a fair packet out of it."

The rest of the day was long and weary. Peter was glad when it came to an end. They might have covered twenty kilometres, but it seemed like fifty.

"We come upon ol' Mac tomorrow," Jet informed him as he pulled some provisions out of his store. Peter ate in silence, and berated himself for being such a fool as to embark on this new way of life.

At present, he was depending for his survival and safety on this young boy, while the future awaiting him when he reached his journey's end did not look very inviting.

He spent a long time pulling the spinifex spines from his legs. They stung where they had penetrated, and he hoped the sores would not fester.

Early in the day he had tried to save his legs and ankles by wrapping them round with his singlets but by midday the singlets looked like pin-cushions, and were so filled with prickles that he knew he could never wear them again. He threw them away and walked more carefully, even though this slowed them up.

The next day was a repetition of the first. By now, he had lost all sense of time and did not even know which day it was. If he had, it would not have mattered. He knew only that if he did not arrive at some place soon, he would just have to sit down and ask Jet to go for help.

He did not say this to the boy, but Jet sensed it.

"You're pretty done in, ain't you, Pete?" he asked.

Peter did not reply, but when Jet slipped down from the horse and told him to mount, he did not refuse.

Fortunately water was no problem, as they kept close to the river and there was a plentiful supply. By now the torrent had passed and the river had dropped in level until it was just a number of disconnected, but well-filled, pools.

About midday, Jet pointed to two clouds of smoke.

"Ol' Mac," he said. "He's closer than I

thought he was. He's calling us to come back to base."

"How? You got a radio?"

"No. He just puts some green on the fire— it can be seen for a great distance. It's our signal. One lot of smoke at midday means for us to go on, two lots to come back."

"There are others?"

"My dad and some uncles."

The conversation languished at this point, while Peter used every nerve and sinew to stay on the horse. Though the smoke had appeared close, it was the middle of the afternoon before Jet gave a grunt and remarked, "We're here."

Peter looked ahead. The river took a curve and on the headland were some large trees. Under the trees he could see two trucks. Jet moved fast and Peter, making a final effort, urged the horse onward. The place was deserted, but assorted gear on the ground showed that it was a place which had been used for a camp for several days.

Peter slipped off the horse and sat down in the shade of one of the trucks. Jet rummaged amongst the stores and made some billy tea.

This time he found another pannikin and he gave this filled with black tea to Peter. If it had been hemlock Peter would have been just as grateful. He gulped down the hot brew with great enjoyment.

His lips were swollen and cracked, his face was sore from the sun and his legs were aching and sore. In all, he was a bundle of misery and felt very sorry for himself.

Fortunately, he was able to rest undisturbed for a few hours and this gave him a little more strength. At about five o'clock there came the sound of cattle and horses. Peter saw a cloud of dust. As it came closer, he noticed that a number of small calves were being driven towards the camp by two Aboriginal stockmen and a broad, middle-sized man, who was alternately cursing the stockmen, the calves, and the dogs which were keeping them going in the right direction.

Jet ran out to help. Peter was too tired to stand up or in fact do anything except just lie where he was. The men were too pre-occupied to notice him, and it was not until the animals had been shut in a rough sort of pen that any of them came towards the truck.

The first to come over was Josh McMichael. As he approached, Peter noticed that he had a huge body, but that his legs were so short that he looked almost grotesque.

He was wiping the sweat from his large, florid face and waving the flies away with a great dirty hand. He was dressed in grey dungarees and a dirty brown shirt, and had a large sweat-rag tied round his neck. As he came closer, Peter noticed he reeked of perspiration.

McMichael came up, stood in front of the boy with one hand on his hip, and said by way of greeting, "Who the bleeding hell are you?"

"Peter Devlin. Mrs Sloan wrote."

"Oh, the city kid. I remember." The fellow removed his hat and scratched his head. "How did you get here? Drop in from the air?"

"No, sir. I came by coach about five days ago."

"Where've you been since?"

"Waiting on the roadside. Mrs Sloan sent a telegram but it's still in your mail-bin."

McMichael burst out laughing. Peter failed to see anything funny in what he had said and remained silent.

"Damn fool city kid—you're lucky to be alive. Did Jet pick you up?"

"Yes. A day or so ago. I managed to get a little water and I had a little food."

The man stood considering. It was apparent that the boy had had a tough few days.

"You look pretty useless to me at present," he commented. "We're about thirty kilometres from the homestead or I'd send you off on a horse, but you might fall off and we'd have to waste time searching for you. Hey, Tom," he called to one of the Aborigines. "Come over here." A tall, slim man slouched over and stood nearby.

"I think I'd better send this fellow back to the house. I didn't intend to send a load in till tomorrow, but you can all give a hand. We'll load up the animals we've got and you can go in tonight. I want you back by sun-up. Come, boy. Lend a hand with the loading. It's on your account."

Peter could well have been spared this exertion, but he made a brave attempt to help. It was with relief that he saw the loading completed. A rough meal was then prepared and about an hour later, just as the sun was going down, the truck set off on its journey to the homestead.

"Make yourself useful until we return," McMichael instructed him. "Tom will show you where to stay. You can use the shearers' hut."

"Me too?" asked Jet.

"No. You stay. You've been away on your walkabout too long already. There's work to do. You find anything?"

"Some clean-skins about twenty kilometres back."

"Good. We'll attend to them tomorrow."

Tom pressed the starter button on the truck, drowning out any further instructions or comments from his boss. They bumped away into the dusk.

Tom was not a communicative man, and after a few minutes Peter stopped trying to draw him out. The driver turned on the headlights, but as only one of them worked, the track ahead was left more to the imagination and the experience of what the driver knew about it than to what he could see. As a result the truck bumped and skidded in the thick dust, while from behind the calves uttered a continual protest.

If Peter had had any muscles which were not aching before the trip, by the end of it these too were as sore as the rest. After two hours or so, suddenly the truck's single headlight picked up some buildings and, driving into the midst of these, Tom announced that they had arrived.

"You help me unload and then you can sleep," he said.

It was pitch dark, but Tom knew where he was. He backed the truck and ordered Peter out. Tom came round the other side, undid the truck's tail gate, and dropped it on to a ramp. Tom and Peter climbed into the truck and pushed and prodded the animals till they stumbled out of the back, down the ramp, and into a pen beyond.

"That will do till morning," Tom informed him. "Get your pack."

Wearily the boy did so and, taking his torch, followed the man. They came to a long building.

"In here," said Tom, flinging a door open.

Peter shone his torch into a small, bare room.

It had a sagging spring-bed without a kapok mattress, a box for a chair, and two boxes for a dressing-table.

He heard the man moving back into the darkness. The boy removed his boots and would have flung himself, clothed as he was, on to the bed, but as his trousers were still full of prickles he took them off and threw them on the floor.

The wire mattress was too rough on him in his thin underpants, and so he took his towel and laid it over the wire. This was a success and he did not remember falling asleep.

Chapter Seven

OPERATION HYGIENE

PETER DREAMED THAT HE WAS gradually being roasted to death in a hot oven, and that he was being beaten with pieces of prickly pear. He gasped for water, and in his struggles rolled off the bed on to the floor.

His dream and reality were not much different, except that, as he picked himself up from the floor, he found himself surrounded by a swarm of flies which were biting his bare legs. The sun was streaming in the open door and the room was as hot as the oven in his dreams.

It was evident he had slept through the morning. He went to the door and looked out.

Some distance away, a large corrugated-iron building shimmered in the heat. Seventy-five metres to his right, a long, low building with a few wool bales lying in front of it proclaimed itself as the shearing shed. Close to him, a low, mean building, with open fireplaces in front, suggested the Aborigines' quarters. Twenty metres away from his door, a shed with a table in it and with a small room attached indicated, he presumed, the shearers' dining-room and kitchen.

Peter was hot, thirsty, and dirty. He put on some clean underwear and a spare pair of trousers from his haversack, found his towel, and walked outside in his bare feet. He did not go more than a few paces on the hot ground before he had to run with great speed back to his room to put his shoes on.

Near the large corrugated-iron building, which he guessed was the homestead, was a windmill and a huge tank. He walked over to it.

Beside the windmill was a crude bath-house. A bucket under a tap was the only equipment inside. There was a small piece of soap on the edge of the stand supporting the tank.

He first of all drank his fill from the tap. He then stripped and, using the bucket, poured the water over him, using the soap, until he felt clean and refreshed. Dressed again, he set out to explore the other buildings.

From the pen where the calves were came their protests. He himself had had a great drink of water, and when he moved over and found their trough dry, he had a feeling of compassion for them.

There was no pipe to their trough and so he had to use the bucket from the crude bath-house to take water over. Before he had finished, he was as hot as when he had first awakened.

There was no sign of life around the collection of buildings. As he walked past the windmill on his last trip back, he flung the bucket towards it and moved over to the homestead.

It was a sprawling affair, with some of its roof torn off on one corner and never replaced —no doubt some cyclone had struck a little harder than usual. He was not sure whether or not he could expect to find anyone inside, and so he approached the place from the front and moved on to the wide verandah. It was sagging a little, but as it was facing south, it provided coolness and shade.

Facing him was a central door with a window on either side. He banged on the door and called out. When it was clear that no one was inside, he pushed the door open.

He found himself in what was apparently the main living-room. A sagging couch, a table covered with dust, a few old chairs, and a kangaroo-skin mat completed its contents. There were no curtains at the dirty windows.

A door to one side led into a bedroom. He peered inside. A sagging double bed, with some dirty sheets tossed on it in a heap, almost filled the room.

A rough wardrobe held a dusty collection of clothes, while a battered dressing-table, with the glass cracked all the way across, was covered with old papers and a weird collection of odds and ends, including several old pipes, packets of tobacco, and an old kerosene lamp.

There was a musty smell about this room and, indeed, about the whole place, which repulsed him. The windows were jammed shut and though the place was lined with a patterned tin lining, the heat inside was still almost overpowering.

Peter moved to another door which led into the kitchen. He was shocked. Great piles of unwashed dishes stood on the central table, a pile of empty cans lay in the corner, and the central stove was covered with grime and grease. The floor had been cemented over, but this too was thick with fat and the discarded mess of many meals. There was a large storeroom, but even here the same carelessness and dirtiness was more than apparent.

Sacks of sugar and flour lay open on the shelves and a cloud of flies rose whenever he moved. In one corner, a hessian water-cooler stood, but it was dry and not in use. Its contents were raising a foul smell. Peter opened the door and found a jug of sour milk and some rancid butter.

For a moment he was overwhelmed by the impulse to turn and run, to escape from the place before McMichael returned. Then commonsense won. At best he would be back where he was before Jet had found him; at worst he would have to remain, at least until he was able to sort things out.

He checked over the rest of the house. None of the other rooms was in use. They were filled with discarded clothes, old boots, and other rubbish.

Old McMichael had written, "This is no palis . . ." It was the most dreadful place Peter had ever seen, even including his former slum-room.

Yet, despite this disgust, the normal demands of a healthy boy were intruding upon him, and he felt very hungry. He looked around in the storeroom until he found some tinned beef. He opened it, and ate it with relish.

His hunger temporarily satisfied, Peter began to consider the situation. It was clear that whether he wanted it or not, he was now going to have to live a very primitive existence, until he could get away from the place. This he might not be able to do for some time.

It would therefore be necessary for him to think of his own welfare first, as apparently McMichael would consider this the least of his worries.

He strolled over to the shearers' quarters and went through the other small rooms to see what he could find to make his own room more comfortable. Behind one door, he was fortunate enough to find a good, wide-brimmed hat which fitted him. It had apparently been left by the last user of the room.

In another room he found a kapok mattress, but when he lifted it, he noticed it was crawling with bedbugs, so he hastily dropped it. Instead he looked around for some sacks to cover the bare wire of his bed.

In a corner he found some of the coarse material used for making the wool bales. He took some back and spread two layers on his bed. He rolled up one piece to make a pillow. At least now he had a clean place to sleep.

Though he did not relish the idea, Peter returned to the homestead. Like it or not, he would probably have to eat his meals there, and perhaps even prepare them. There was one thing he could do, though whether or not it would meet with McMichael's approval he did not know, and that was to clean up the kitchen.

Outside the back door, a great pile of wood and tree roots had been unloaded. He collected as much as he could get and set the fire going in the stove. The fat on top soon caught alight, and the kitchen filled with smoke and heat, but it was a much more pleasant smell than it had been before.

Then he filled every pot, pan, and kettle he could find with water, and placed them on the top of the stove. While he was waiting for them to boil, he removed the rotting food from the cooler, found some cleaning material and washed the tin trays.

He had read of such coolers; his grandfather had told him how in the early days they used them in the goldfields. They consisted of a steel frame surrounded by hessian, with a large tray on top to hold water. Pieces of rag conducted the water to the hessian sides down which it ran to another tray on the bottom. As the water evaporated from the damp hessian the air around was cooled. The overflow then dripped into a container which could be taken out and emptied into the top tray for the water to do its job again.

He had noticed what might be a cool area on the front verandah and he moved the whole thing outside, setting it up on a box and filling its upper tray with water. He was pleased to notice the hessian becoming wet.

By now the pans of water were boiling, and he set them down on the floor. As the smoke from the top of the stove was annoying him, he went outside, found a piece of tin and scraped the top, until eventually, as a result of his efforts from above and the heat of the flames from beneath, the clean iron showed through, and what was more, the kitchen became clear of smoke.

It was too hot to work in his clothing, and so he stripped to his singlet and underpants. He wished that he had his case at hand so that he could get some shorts, but he felt very much cooler with the removal of his outer garments. Eventually he even took off his singlet, more with the thought that everything he made dirty now he would have to wash, than to cool himself further.

He began with the table, and was surprised to find that it did not resist his efforts but came up to a fair state of cleanliness, with patches of white showing through. For good measure he washed the sides and legs.

The floor was a different proposition, but he had noticed some soap powder in a cupboard and he applied it liberally, pouring on the hot water. He had long since removed his boots and as he stood up, after a very determined effort on the floor, his legs suddenly shot from under him and he went sprawling in the mess of suds and grease.

He arrived against the far wall with a bang, having skidded the entire length of the kitchen. Until then he had tackled the job with grim determination, but when, breathless, soapy, and greasy, he picked himself up his natural good humour came back to him, and he giggled stupidly.

The mishap made him pause. He realised that he was tackling the job too grimly and that he must not do that. Taking a rag, he dipped it into the hot water and, when it was cool enough, wiped himself clean.

Then he went to the store, found some tea, some sugar, and some powdered milk and, washing out a pannikin from the dirty dishes, made a good brew. He found some biscuits in a cupboard and ate half the packet. Life improved immediately.

It took him the rest of the day to complete all he wanted to do in the kitchen and storeroom, but when he had finished, he stood back and admired his handiwork. He had been so engrossed in it that time, the heat of the day, and all else, seemed to pass over him unnoticed.

Once during the day he heard a truck. When he went out to investigate, he saw Tom attending to the feeding of the calves. This done, Tom jumped in the truck and drove off again in a cloud of dust.

Peter enjoyed going through the storeroom. Though things were in total disarray, there was no stint to the amount of food available. He found the proper bins for the sugar and flour, stacked the cans according to their contents, and packed the other things, including the large cardboard boxes holding a dozen bottles of beer each, in neat stacks under the shelves. He found some tinned butter and put this in the cooler, together with a fresh jug of powdered milk.

Peter decided that if there was time, he would begin on the living-room the next day. In the meantime he made some scones in the oven, opened some more tinned meat, and finished his meal with some canned fruit.

When night fell, he lit the kerosene lamp. It needed attention, both to the wick and the glass. When this was done, it shone brightly. He searched the house and in one of the rooms found another lamp.

It too needed attention, but when he had found a new wick for it, it gave a good light. He took it to his room. He was not sure that McMichael would sanction this luxury, and so he intended to make sure of it himself.

He also took a screw-top tin, filled it with kerosene, and hid it in his quarters.

In the main room, a pile of newspapers and old magazines gave him something to read before he felt tired enough to go to bed. He went quite early, well pleased with himself and his day's work.

Chapter Eight

PETER TALKS WITH A MAN

WHEN HE AWOKE NEXT MORNING, he found Jet standing at the door peering in on him.

"Going to sleep all day?"

"No. When did you come in?"

"Last night with some cattle. Drove them down."

"Anyone come back with you?"

"Ol' Mac says they'll all be in by the end of the week."

"End of the week? What day is it now?"

"Dunno. Doesn't matter anyway. Ol' Mac wants us to go out and bring in sheep."

"What for?"

"Shearing of course."

"In the middle of summer?"

"Yep. Ol' Mac shears all the year round. He gets us to bring in sheep whenever we find them, and when he has enough he gets a shearer out to do them over."

"Must be pretty expensive that way."

"No. Cheaper. Most of the blokes have spent

their money in the pub by now, and they can do with a little to see them through. They come pretty cheap in the summer."

Peter pulled his clothes on, and together they went down to the house.

Jet's eyes opened when he saw the clean kitchen.

"Who done this?"

"Me."

"I don't think Mac will like it—too clean. He's a pig."

"How would you know?"

Jet looked at him with hurt in his eyes. Peter had put too much emphasis on the "you."

Jet plucked his brown arm, showing his fine skin.

"Does that make me a pig too, or stop me from knowing when someone is a pig?"

"I'm sorry. I really didn't mean it that way."

"No! You think I always live like this?"

"I wouldn't know," said Peter defensively. "I hadn't thought about it."

"Well, maybe I got ideas, too. You ain't the only city boy. I used to live there once."

"Come on," said Peter. "We'll forget about it. We've both come down in the world."

Jet laughed.

"Too true when you come to Boolgana."

Peter made breakfast. He did not ask the other boy if he had eaten, but made enough for two. Jet took it without comment, but ate with enjoyment.

"First I'll go out and get you a horse. You'll find a saddle in the shearing shed. Go get it."

Peter found an old saddle and brought it back to the house. Jet was away longer than he expected, and so he replenished the water in the cooler and began to clean up the living-room. He had just scrubbed the floor when the other boy returned.

Outside the sun was hot, but with his big, newly acquired hat, Peter could stand it. He found another water-bottle the same size as Jet's, and filled it from the tank.

They rode five kilometres south from the homestead and began to cast about. In about two hours they had about ten sheep which they drove back to pens alongside the sheds.

"That will do for today," said Jet. "Tomorrow we get plenty from the river."

Peter looked at him. "We don't seem to have done much for the day."

"Plenty for the pay we'll get. I'm off for a sleep."

"Have something to eat?"

"No. Only eat morning and evening. You'd better get used to it too."

Peter was hungry and so he ignored the boy's advice. He found himself a soft spot on the sagging couch and spent a little time reading.

It was too hot to lie around and so, after a while, he continued his self-appointed task of cleaning. There was little more he could do in the main room and so he tried the bedroom, but after setting the bed straight and sweeping the floor he left it, defeated by the lack of anywhere to put anything, and the sickly smell.

He was lonely and so he decided to seek out Jet. Putting on his hat, he moved over to the small building which he had noticed the first time he had surveyed the homestead and its surroundings.

He peered into two of the rooms but found them empty. In the third Jet lay asleep on a blanket, having cast off most of his rough clothes. Peter was surprised to see how young the boy really looked. His features were more European than Aboriginal, and he looked to Peter rather like a Spanish boy he had known at school.

"Poor little devil," he thought, "wonder what will happen to him." Suddenly he was aware that the eyes were open, looking up at him.

"Want something?"

"No, but I was lonely and wanted someone to talk to."

"I ain't much to talk to."

"You're a pretty nice kid. You're not very old are you?"

"Plenty. I'm a man."

Peter laughed. "I'm older than you and I don't consider myself a man yet."

"It's different with us. The tribe made me one."

"Wasn't too pleasant?"

"Hurt a bit, but it changed things."

"How do you mean?"

"Made me think differently. When I was in the city I thought like you. Now I think like them."

Peter noticed the use of "you" and "I" and "them." The boy avoided any suggestion of race, but it was there just the same. Peter knew he was on delicate ground.

"There's nothing to be ashamed of, in 'thinking like them.'"

"No. But it makes a difference. I wanted to go back to the city, but after they done me I felt different. I didn't want to be done—"

"You mean initiated?"

"I mean being made a man their way. But when they made me a man, they made me one of them again."

"Didn't you want to go back to the city?"

"Dunno. But it was different."

"Don't you want to have much to do with me? I think you're a nice kid and we've got to work together."

"You're okay, but you're not a man like me. I know more than you."

Peter did not smile or argue. They would not be arguing on a common basis. Instead he said, "I'm a bit of a mug round here. I hope you do know more than me or I'll be in plenty of trouble."

"Nick off," said Jet suddenly. "Nick off."

For a moment Peter thought he was telling him to go. Then he realised. "You mean I ought to go away from here?"

"Fast. It's no good."

"It's good enough for you?"

"That's different. We can make do. We can go when we want. You can't."

"I have nowhere to go. I wouldn't even have my fare back to the city."

"You'll get no good."

"That's a funny way of putting it. Have you 'got no good'?"

"I'm different to you."

"This is where we came in. You're different, you're a man, I'm a boy." Peter was being sarcastic, but Jet failed to see and nodded at each statement.

"Yes. Yes. That's all true. Now nick off."

This time Jet was really dismissing him from his presence.

"Why, you—" Peter began, but then turned and moved back to his room.

For a moment he resented the rudeness of the boy, but then suddenly realised that Jet was right. He, Peter Devlin, was the intruder, and Peter Devlin, the boy, had been dismissed as an inferior by Jet, the man.

If he wanted Jet's friendship, he knew now it would have to be on a different basis from what he had imagined. In this place Jet had more to show him than he could show Jet. There was no equality here. He was just the city kid—a not very great asset in this country.

"I'm caught here," he reflected, "and there's absolutely nothing I can do about it."

Chapter Nine

JOE TURNS UP

PETER HAD JUST DECIDED to prepare an early tea when he became aware that something was coming down the main track from the road. A huge cloud of dust rose in the air, and it was only when the vehicle, or whatever it was, was almost at the station, that the boy could get any indication of its type, size, or shape.

The noise and clatter stopped. Out of the dust, where it had come to a standstill, there emerged one of the oldest, weirdest-looking vehicles that Peter had ever seen.

It was a large four-door car with a bleached canvas roof. Its original colour had long been lost beneath the thick coating of dust. It had no windscreen and no headlights, nor any visible licence plates.

Where the back seat should have been, it was laden with an assortment of gear which had spilled over into the front seat, ready to engulf the driver, if he pulled up too quickly. Along its running boards, it had an assortment of jerrycans tied on with rope. Towed behind it was a trailer on which was a shearing outfit, complete with engine and shearing heads.

This strange vehicle had stopped in front of the shearers' quarters, and Peter moved over. A short, bushy little man stepped out of the car. "Bushy" was the word. His legs, below a pair of tattered shorts, were covered with a mass of black hair, as were his arms, beneath a short-sleeved shirt. He had huge bushy eyebrows and a bushy moustache. His hair stood up in a mass above his forehead.

Aroused by the clatter and noise, Jet had also appeared.

"'Lo, Joe," he called out. "Did you bring the mail down?"

"Yep," and he pointed to the back of his car, "and a case for a bloke named Devlin."

Sitting on the top of the load was Peter's suitcase. He had not expected to see it ever again.

"I'm Peter Devlin. Thanks a lot."

"I'm Joe Wilson. Found your note, but couldn't find you down the river."

"No. Jet rescued me a few days back. I made it safely."

"The old man here?"

"No," put in Jet. "Won't be back for a bit. We've got a few sheep as starters for you. Didn't think you'd be here so soon."

"You'd better get out and bring in enough to keep me going, fellow."

"There's ten there now," said Peter.

"Ten!" yelled the man. "I don't start till you've got two hundred."

"Okay, keep your hair on," from Jet. "There's plenty down the river. We'll fetch them in tomorrow."

"You want something to eat?" asked Peter. "I was just going to get tea at the house."

"What! Me eat over there? First, old Mac wouldn't like it, and secondly, neither would I. I'm particular where I eat."

"It's different now," said Peter, "I've cleaned it up."

"You what! Mac definitely won't like that either, but this I must see."

He walked over to the homestead, with Peter a few paces behind, and Jet, with a great grin, a few paces ahead.

Jet swept the door open. "Welcome to the Boolgana Hotel."

Joe peered inside, his face registering incredulous surprise. He walked through the door and looked into the kitchen, and his mouth dropped open.

"Cor-r-r! Old Mac's sure going to get a shock."

He walked back to the front door, pausing at the bedroom door.

"You didn't make much impression in there," he remarked. "He'll soon have that room back to normal."

"You make it sound as if the man is hopeless," Peter put in.

"He is, as you'll see for yourself, if you last that long after he sees what you've done to his sty."

Joe moved out back towards his quarters. Peter joyfully retrieved his case and took it to his room. Jet followed, leaning against the door-post and watching him as he opened the lid and examined its contents.

Jet's eyes widened, and Peter could see he was gazing at a tie-dyed shirt which he had inherited from Ian Sloan. On a sudden impulse, Peter flung it to him.

"It's yours."

Jet took it with evident delight, but made no comment.

"Don't you say thanks?"

"No. My mob always share."

"My mob always say thanks."

Jet flung the shirt back and stalked out.

Peter grinned to himself. Round three coming up with the honours even . . .

Outside Joe was unloading. Peter shut the case and went outside to help.

He indicated the room with its shoddy furnishings and mattress full of bedbugs.

Joe laughed. "You'll get used to them in this job. We'll pull the mattress out and paint both it and the bed with kerosene. That will fix them."

"Mr McMichael won't like it," said Peter with a grin.

"To blazes with him," was the reply. "If he gets too difficult we'll blacklist him and he'll never get a shearer near the place."

"You must be pretty hard up to come here," said Peter.

"No. Not me. It's just that I don't like sitting around doing nothing until the season comes along. I do all right."

"Would you like me to get you something to eat?"

"Mightn't be a bad idea, sonny. I'll sling you a few dollars for yourself, if you look after me well enough."

"I wasn't doing it for that—"

"If you wasn't, you're a bigger fool than you look."

"Thanks."

The shearers' kitchen was in much better condition than that in the main house, and it was not long before Peter had a stew cooking from the provisions Joe had given him. He had begun to like the rough character, and felt at home with him.

Joe had brought his own kerosene lamps, and

after tea he wanted to sit yarning with Peter and with Jet, who had come to visit. It was hard to guess how old he was—any age from forty to sixty, Peter decided. He had a natural bushman's ability for telling a good story with plenty of embellishments and laced with spicy language. Peter enjoyed it all immensely, and the man, sensing this, played up to the boy's appreciation.

He had a sly way of intruding a fact and, when it was not challenged, adding to it, until eventually one or other of his listeners became incredulous and challenged him, with the result that he would stop, pause for a moment, and after a slow wink, remark, "You wouldn't be doubting my veracity, would you?"

"I wouldn't know," Jet remarked on one occasion, "but I reckon you're lying."

At this, the fellow jumped to his feet, adopting a fighting stance, and remarked, "Those who doubt Joe Wilson had better back it with action."

"Would knocking me down prove you tell the truth?"

Joe burst out laughing.

"You got a ready tongue on you, Jet my boy. Likely as not you'll end up a politician."

"Not me. My father would shoot me. Don't hold with that lot. He says they give him the right to drink without landing in the jug, and then take taxes out of his wages for the privilege."

"Neatly put," agreed Joe, "even if you have got a bit mixed up. Come on—help me clean up this mess, so I can get to bed."

Peter went to his room that night feeling that, come what may, while Joe was around he had a friend to help him along. He had an idea that Jet rather admired Joe, too.

Chapter Ten

CYCLONE

NEXT DAY, VERY EARLY in the morning, Jet dragged Peter out of bed.

"Come on. We've got to get the sheep to keep Joe going."

"How many does he need?"

"About a hundred a day. He'll have to put through a few thousand to make coming out here worthwhile."

"Can we find that many?"

"We'll be scraping a bit at the end, but the others will be in by then and they'll help."

For the first day or so, Joe worked only in the afternoon and waited till the boys came in. He appeared to be in no hurry, but to be awaiting the return of McMichael and the two stockmen.

In the meantime he used the boys as the rouse-abouts, roughly classing the wool himself, calling a number on each fleece. Peter then flung the fleece in the appropriate bin, on which Joe had placed the appropriate number. It was crude and unsatisfactory, but it had to do. The shorn sheep were allowed to wander down the ramp and to find their own way back to the river.

At midday on the third day McMichael returned to the homestead. He saw the activity at the shed and came over, nodding his head with appreciation but saying nothing.

As the old man moved in the direction of the house, Joe turned the engine off.

"It is going to be funny," he said, "when old Mac finds his pretty new home."

It wasn't really. There was a roar from the house as McMichael emerged, his face red with anger, and came running on his short little legs towards the shed.

"Where's that blasted boy?" he yelled. "Who told you to go mucking about in the house?"

"I thought you'd like it cleaned up a bit," Peter yelled back. "It was pretty untidy, Mr McMichael."

"Are you saying you had the cheek to go and muck round in my house without my permission? Who do you think you are? This ain't the city, and if I want to live rough, I'll live rough."

"You mean, Mac," Joe put in, "if you want to pig it, you'll pig it."

"Shut up," yelled McMichael. "I wasn't talking to you."

"But I was to you, you old buzzard. The boy did what he thought was right. You can't blame him for that. He must have been pretty game, even to go into your stinking house."

McMichael decided to ignore Joe.

"Listen, boy," he said, "you don't do nothing round here unless I say so. You understand? You just keep out of my house."

"Where do I eat?"

"Take your pick, with Jet and his pa, or with your great friend, Joe Wilson here. If you work, you can draw your rations with the rest."

Peter felt it was no time to argue.

"I'm sorry, Mr McMichael. I'll do my best."

The man turned and moved back to his house.

"Rotten old sod," said Joe. "One day he'll go too far and then he'll be in the soup."

With the return of McMichael, however, a little more order returned to the woolshed. Jet's father and uncle kept up a good supply of sheep to the shed, and while Jet acted as rouse-about, Peter concentrated on the skirtings. With only one shearer it was not hard work for the boys.

McMichael proved to be a morose and taciturn man. Try as he could, Peter could get no response except rudeness from him, and in the end gave up trying to make contact. Years of living by himself, eking out a hard living, had made the man what he was, and there was no changing him.

Strangely enough Peter was not unhappy.

He found the heat overpowering at first, but gradually adapted to it. Apparently he was earning his rations, for McMichael put them out regularly with those for Jet and the other two. Joe did not need any as he was entirely self-sufficient.

Peter undertook looking after Joe, kept his room tidy, did all the cooking he wanted, and listened to Joe talk night after night. It seemed to be an existence to which there was no end. Then Jet sounded a warning.

"You'd better get a move on, Joe, if you want to make your money this time. The weather is going to break pretty soon."

Peter looked surprised.

"Just my luck," said Joe. "There's been little enough round these parts for the past few years and then we get a cyclone."

"Cyclone?" asked Peter. "What do you mean?"

"Only cyclonic weather penetrates this far inland," explained Joe. "By then most of its force is blown out and we just get the rain that goes with it, but now and again we get a real buster."

"But how do you know the weather is going to break?"

"There're plenty of signs, but you wouldn't see them," interrupted Jet.

"You think you're plenty smart, don't you?"

said Peter, incensed by the boy's continual desire to prove his superiority.

"Let him be," interposed Joe. "He's got little enough to crow about. You'll never make a team while you carry on that way."

"A team?" queried Jet.

"Yep. You could both learn plenty from each other, if you weren't both so touchy."

Both boys remained silent. Then Peter said, "He needles me."

"He gets my goat," said Jet, expressing it equally as well.

"You'll both get a good boot in the tail if you go on this way," put in Joe. "Now get on with your work."

One person had no doubt that the weather was going to break. This was Josh McMichael. This became evident when, instead of letting the shorn sheep trail back to the river as they had been doing, he had Tom keep them in a holding-pen. When there were enough, he had them driven off to a windmill, some ten kilometres on the other side of the river.

He in turn scoured the river-flats, and with the aid of his dogs drove all the sheep he could find to the yards around the house and shearing sheds.

These trips outward took a long time, but when he was assigned to go out, even Peter noticed a change in the weather. First there was a purple tinge to the hitherto blue sky, which gradually gave way to a few clouds high in the sky. Then, in the far distance, on the horizon, a low line of black clouds appeared which, when they had advanced, shut out the sun completely and made the air hot and sticky.

The next day the whole sky was dark grey, and there seemed to be a general air of uneasiness over all the countryside.

A large mob of sheep had been assembled, which McMichael wanted driven out to the ten-kilometre mill. Every dog on the station was called into action and both boys were ordered to help as well.

Jacky Windmill and Tom Tomahawk were good drovers, but the sheep seemed uneasy and Peter doubted whether their progress was more than two kilometres an hour.

They crossed the Dankin River, which gave little evidence of its recent flooding. The sheep would have preferred to have stayed there, and it was with difficulty that they could be driven onward.

There was not a breath of air, and the dust from the animals rose slowly but did not blow away. As a result, Peter found himself choking and had to reach constantly for his water-bottle.

They had been several hours on their journey when the wind came. At first it raised various clouds of dust in parts of the country lying around them, but soon it ceased to be gusty and blew quite strongly in their faces.

Peter found this very uncomfortable and tied a handkerchief over his nose like a mask. As the wind grew stronger it blew up quite large particles of sand and grit, which stung the face and any exposed skin.

Soon it was so strong and so constant that Peter caught only occasional glimpses of the others. The sheep wanted to turn their rumps to the onslaught, but for a little while the pressure of the men, the boys, and the dogs was enough to keep them moving forward.

Then the horses themselves refused to move forward. Peter found his horse moving sideways to the blast, and then it finally stopped altogether.

A dim form came up alongside him. It was Jet.

"Come on," he yelled. "Follow me."

As he said so, the clouds opened, and in a second the blinding, stinging dust storm gave way to a mass of blinding, stinging water that took even the horse unaware. It slipped, flinging Peter on to the ground. Before he could grasp its bridle, it had made off back in the direction of the river.

Jet seemed to sense what had happened for, as Peter rose with difficulty to his feet, the indistinct form of the boy and his horse came for a second into Peter's sight, and he ran and grasped the stirrup nearest to him.

Peter had lost all sense of direction, but Jet appeared to be trying to urge his horse onward. Peter clung to the saddle, aware that the storm now appeared to bear on their backs, but with so much intensity that it was impossible to see even a metre in front of them. Speech was impossible, but though the horse seemed to want to move forward faster, Jet was holding it back, so that Peter would be able to keep up with it.

A number of times it seemed as if they would be blown to the ground by the fury of the storm, but miraculously the horse and the two boys kept going—just in what direction, and for what purpose, Peter had no idea.

Once or twice there was a brief lull in the wind but the rain continued to pour down, as if from a million buckets.

They had proceeded in this fashion for what seemed like hours to Peter, when suddenly he found they were descending a steep slope. As they did so, the fury of the gale from behind them diminished, and Peter was able to observe that the deep trench made by the river was acting as a protection to them.

The great blasts seemed to skim over the top of the cutting, leaving a small area where, protected by the bank, they could move for shelter, if not from the rain, at least from the terrific wind which went with it. The noise of the elements was still ear-shattering.

Peter could see that Jet was moving them down to the river-bed. A rift in the rock allowed them a small place to stand, where they were free of both the driving rain and the wind.

Dismounting, Jet yelled in Peter's ear, "We can stay here for a while, but we may be flooded out. Listen."

Peter assumed Jet meant him to listen for any signs of the river's coming down, but how he would do so with the great roar of the wind and rain already at a crescendo, he did not know.

Then suddenly, almost before they knew it, the water was upon them. It did not come down in the great wall that the boys had experienced before, but rose from the river-bed, first round their ankles, and then up to their knees.

Jet recognised the danger at once.

"Get on the horse," he yelled as he jumped back into the saddle.

Peter did not argue, but mounted behind him. Jet turned the horse's head, directing it to cross to the other side of the river. The water was still shallow enough for it to do so, but was rising fast.

The horse slipped and floundered but somehow reached the other side, and they urged it up the other bank. The water, as if to make a final effort, suddenly surged up behind them, over the top of the bank, and the horse rolled over.

Peter tumbled beneath the water, but struck out and came to the surface, to see Jet being swept by. He grabbed the boy, who was kicking wildly.

They were swept against a tree and missed its branches. They fended themselves off another, but could gain no hand-hold on it. Before them a low branch dipped into the water. Peter made a grab for it. Jet grabbed and missed.

Peter again caught him as he was swept by, and Jet, with almost a superhuman effort, hauled himself back along Peter, and was able to grasp the branch for himself. He swung himself on to it, pulling an exhausted Peter up with him.

The water was still rising fast, and so they scrambled along the branch to the main trunk and moved higher up the tree. Circumstances had been kind to them. By chance they had come up against one of the largest trees on the river-bank.

"We'll be safe enough," said Jet, sizing up the situation, "but we may have to sit it out for a few days."

"What happened to the horse?" Peter asked.

Jet pointed. It had made safety, on one of the

very few ridges which cut across the country, and which now stuck up like a peninsula in a sea of water.

At that moment the storm struck again, and for the next few hours the boys had hard work to stop themselves from being blown into the water below. They were fearful that at any moment the tree itself might be blown over, being sure that if it did, they would not survive a second time.

Chapter Eleven

JOE TO THE RESCUE

BY NIGHTFALL THE CYCLONE had blown itself out. By then, both Peter and Jet had managed to get themselves into a secure position, but they were wet, cold, and shivering. When the rain finally stopped, Peter tried to wring as much water out of his clothes as possible. He knew that they were both in a very dangerous situation and that unless someone found them the next day, the chances of their survival were slim.

The long weary hours of the night went by. At the beginning the boys tried to talk to each other, but by morning there were long periods of silence, broken by one or the other calling out to make sure they were both still in the tree.

At daybreak, a watery sun shone through the broken clouds in the sky and gave a little warmth. They looked to the peak where the horse had been the night before. There was no sign of it.

"The water isn't too deep," Jet said, "but it's too strong for us to swim through. Otherwise we could make our way to where the horse was. If we followed the ridge we could get back to Boolgana. The water would be about waist high."

"We'd never make it," said Peter. "How long will the river be up?"

"Could be days. Depends on how far inland this storm went. It will get deeper round here, before it runs off, when the flood from upriver comes down."

The chill of the night and the frightening experiences of the cyclone disturbed Peter greatly. Jet did not seem concerned outwardly, though he was shivering.

Suddenly Jet said, "Listen!"

Peter strained his ears, but could hear nothing.

"It's Joe," said Jet. "He's coming out in the car."

"With water-wings?" interjected Peter.

"No, I can hear him. He'll find us. Don't worry. Joe's a good bloke."

Peter strained his ears but could hear nothing at first. Then faintly he heard the blowing of a motor horn. Joe had a great bulb horn on his car and someone was honking it continually.

It was not till some time later that Peter was able to hear the sound of an engine a long way off. He searched the wide stretch of water now lying between them and the homestead, but could see nothing.

"Joe's smart," said Jet. "He'll keep to the high ground. If he hurries he can just about arrive before the main flood comes down."

About five minutes later Jet saw the car. It was not coming directly, but was moving across the country, apparently on the continuation of the ridge on which the horse had found safety. Looking in that direction, Peter noticed that already the area of high ground they had seen the night before had almost vanished under the rising water.

Soon they were able to distinguish things more clearly. Moving through the sea of water, Tom Tomahawk was riding a horse ahead of the car, carefully feeling the way, and for security was carrying a long rope linking him to the car itself.

Joe was driving very carefully. Already water was up to the doors of the vehicle, but as it was one of the old vehicles which were built high off the ground, it could go even deeper in the water before its engine was affected.

After a few precarious minutes it emerged from the water, and Joe cut off the engine as he brought it on to the one small patch of dry ground near the tree where the boys were marooned.

Joe began to honk his horn continually and the boys had to hold back their yells until he stopped. Even then it was some five minutes before they were located.

Tom was the first to pin-point the tree. As the boys watched, they saw Joe gesticulating and it was evident he was suggesting that the stockman edge his horse down to them. Another figure had emerged from the back of the car. It was Jet's father.

The two men, using the car as an anchor, payed out the rope gradually, while the man on the horse made his way slowly to them. For a few moments it looked as if the manoeuvre might be successful, but suddenly the horse slipped and was swept out of their sight downstream. The men at the car hauled the rider back, where the boys saw him crawl, wet and shaken, out of the water, while the others checked him for injury.

Apparently he had suffered no damage and as they watched, they saw the three busily engaged in some other activity at the car. Peter was beginning to realise that their chance of rescue now appeared very slim.

As they watched, they saw that Joe was apparently blowing up a large inner tyre tube. When he had finished, they saw the others taking a coil of rope from inside the car.

"They're going to try and float a line down

to us," said Peter. "They'll have to hurry. The water is still rising."

A few minutes later the tube was thrown into the water and, as the men let the line out, it was swept in their direction. It came nearer and nearer, but it was apparent that it would miss the tree by at least six metres.

The men hauled it in again, and this time Jet's father took it and, wading closer to the river and ahead of the car, threw it as far out as he could.

This time it was clear that the tube would float under one of the branches of the tree. Jet scrambled down to get to it. Between him and the main trunk, a huge brown snake barred the way.

"A blasted Joe Blake," Jet yelled to Peter. "Get me a stick."

"You'll have to take a chance," Peter yelled back. "Drop on to the tube and hang on. There's nothing I can break off here to dislodge the snake."

Jet paused for a moment.

"What about you. You go first."

"Don't argue," Peter returned. "I can swim better than you. Now be careful. Drop carefully."

It was not a time for argument. The boy swung under the branch and launched himself at the tube. Though he had not planned it that way, he went through its middle, and it circled him like a lifebelt, when he surfaced.

"Pull!" yelled Peter. "Pull!"

The others hauled on the rope. In a few minutes they had pulled Jet safely back to the car.

Then they repeated the operation, though this time it was Joe who dropped the line down. The water had risen to such a degree that he took a line from the car to use if the water, now up to his arm-pits, should prove too strong for him.

Again the tube lay beneath the tree. Peter swung himself down the branch and dropped.

In his eagerness to make sure he landed on the tube, Peter miscalculated and swung out too far. He hit the water and went under, but his groping hands failed to find the floating object on which his life depended. He flailed round, and in his struggles suddenly found his arm entangled in the rope.

He moved his other hand over and grabbed it, and then managed to get a grip with his first hand, while he sorted out what had happened. He had landed upstream of the tube, and by careful manipulation he slid along the rope, until he was able to put one foot through the tube.

At that moment Joe, feeling the weight on the other end, began to pull lustily, and nearly tore the rope and the tube away. Peter got his knees up and hung on grimly.

He knew that he was being dragged into the shallow water, as he could feel the bottom now and again, and soon the sharp spines of the spinifex began to dig into his back. Letting the tube go, he tried to drop his feet so that he would not be such a dead weight on the line.

In this way he was dragged, like a fish, up on to the area near the car. Joe rushed over and helped him to his feet.

"Thanks, Joe," he managed to stammer.

"Save it," called Joe above the roar of the water. "We ain't home yet. Lend a hand to get this rope back in the car, while I turn her round."

Peter noticed that already the water was lapping the bottoms of the wheels of the vehicle. While he and Jet coiled the rope, Joe, under the direction of one of the stockmen, began the precarious task of trying to turn the car round in the limited space available.

With the loss of the horse, it was evident that someone would have to go out in front to make sure the car stayed on the high ground. Jet's father took a rope and, after tying it to the front bumper, moved ahead some ten metres or so into the deeper water.

Peter and Jet flung the tube on to the roof of the car and then jumped into the back of the vehicle. They watched anxiously as Jack Windmill moved slowly ahead. The car had started up with a great roar and, keeping it in low gear, Joe was able to go at a slow enough pace to allow Windmill to seek out the best way back.

Once or twice the man suddenly submerged to his armpits, and Joe slammed on the brakes. On these occasions, working round to right or left, the man refound the high ground.

On one occasion when this happened Joe called out, "Cut out the swimming practice, Jacky."

To this the man replied good humouredly, "Swap you places."

"Not me," yelled Joe back. "Never stop a man when he's doing a good job."

"Then shut up," yelled Windmill, "and let me get on with it."

They had proceeded a long way in this manner, and indeed the station buildings could just be seen in the distance, when from behind them came a deeper roar than previously.

"It's the main flood," yelled Tom Tomahawk. "You'll have to get moving, Joe."

Joe yelled to the man in the water to come into the car.

"We'll have to take our chance for the rest of the way," he shouted. "We'll be safe at the station; it's never been under water."

He put his foot down on the accelerator and the old vehicle leapt forward, splashing water in all directions, but chugging away with its powerful motor as if it was designed for this sort of work.

"Step on it, Joe," yelled Jet, "the tide's coming in. We're still on the flood-plain and it can get pretty deep here when the main flood comes down."

Joe needed no urging. The car panted, pounded, and shook wildly as it continued its way, like some grotesque marine monster, spraying water in all directions and steaming and smoking as some of it poured over the engine.

Joe hung on to the steering wheel praying that he would not hit some fence or obstruction, while Peter, fearful of looking behind to see if the river was rising, was equally fearful of looking ahead, lest he would glimpse something which would obstruct their passing and bring them to disaster.

Then suddenly the splashing ceased. They had reached the dry area and roared over it with even greater speed, now that they were not impeded by the water.

It was well they had moved so fast, for the rising water pursued them for a further hundred metres. Then suddenly they were beyond its reach. Joe slipped the car into top gear and they sped towards the station buildings, now not very far away.

"Phew," said Joe, "I wouldn't like to repeat that little lot."

Peter and Jet, wet, cold, and weary, could not have agreed more.

Chapter Twelve

GOOD-BYE JOE

THERE WAS NO SIGN of Josh McMichael when they returned to the station and so, after leaving the boys, Joe swung off to look for him, to see if he needed a hand. The two stockmen went to the stables, and without changing their clothes saddled two horses, intending also to try to drive back to the station area any stock which might have been forced to the high ground by the floods.

Peter dropped his wet clothes on the floor, gave himself a rub over with a towel, and then dressed in dry clothing.

Apparently McMichael and Joe had moved in different directions, for Peter saw the car returning at the same time as McMichael rode in with his dogs, driving a large flock of sheep ahead of him. The man stopped when he saw the boy.

"Did you get the sheep to the ten-kilometre mill?"

"Pretty nearly, Mr McMichael."

"Eh! What do you mean by pretty nearly?"

"We lost them in the dust. I don't know what happened to the stockmen, but Jet and I got caught in the dust, and then the rains came."

"Lot of good-for-nothings," roared the man. "The stockman lost the lot of you and came back. He found your horses were here, but you weren't. How a fellow is to know what goes on is something I'll never find out."

"We nearly got drowned."

"So what? You have to learn to look after yourselves. They went off looking for you without my permission this morning."

"Good thing they did," said Peter with spirit, "or we'd be dead by now."

"You trying to make me cry or something?"

"No, but you don't get cyclones like this every day. You shouldn't have sent us out with the weather about to break."

"You trying to tell me?"

"Yes. It wasn't any fun and for all you care we might have got washed away."

By now Joe had arrived in his car and he came into the yard, cut his engine, and stepped out.

"The kids were mighty lucky, Mac," he said. "We just got to them in time. We lost you a horse."

"You what?" screamed the man. "I told you not to go out."

Joe stood there flabbergasted. Then his anger rose.

"You miserable old sod," he yelled. "You put more value on a blasted horse than on these kids."

"It's a lot more useful round here than they have ever been," the man yelled back.

"I ought to shoot you, you rotten old buzzard," cried Joe. "Except it'd be wasting a good bullet. Give me any more of that and I'll make sure you won't have a shearer on the place, or anyone so much as picking up your mail and stores."

McMichael stopped short in the middle of what he was going to yell out next, and said instead, "You wouldn't dare, Wilson."

"Like to call my bluff?"

The old man stood glaring for a moment and then strode off to the house.

"Come on, Peter," Joe called, "I can't do anything for a few days, either leave the place or continue shearing. You must be pretty hungry. We'll get us some grub."

The man and the boy moved off to their quarters, where they were joined by Jet a few minutes later. McMichael stayed sulking in his house for the next twenty-four hours.

In the next two days there were short spells of rain, but it was apparent that the weather was going to clear. Constant inspection showed that the overflow from the river had not made any further encroachments on to the station area.

Joe had set up a stick marking the farthest progress of the river, and on the morning of the third day Peter saw that the water level had dropped greatly. During the next day the water continued to drop noticeably, and long causeways of land began to appear.

When it was safe enough, Joe set off in his trusty car and found that one of these dried-off areas would allow the sheep caught in the station area to be driven along it to higher ground which had not been affected by the flood.

When the sheep had dried out enough, he put those needing shearing through the shed, and then had Jet and the rest drive them off along the way he had found. This kept Peter very busy, but he wondered all the time what would happen when McMichael reappeared.

This he did as large as life next morning, issuing orders as if nothing had happened.

"I'll stay until I get this little lot off my hands," said Joe, indicating the sheep close to the station, many of them still unshorn, "and then I'm off."

Peter was at a loss. When Joe went he was sure he would take him with him, but as Joe himself had said, "What then?"

Peter did not have an answer. Unless McMichael actually kicked him off the place or refused him rations, this was the only place he could stay where he had a roof overhead and regular food.

He had accumulated a little cash reserve. Most of the money Mrs Sloan had given him was unspent, he had the few dollars Ian had given him, and he had a little more that Joe had slung him for preparing his meals and keeping his quarters clean.

McMichael could not be expected to contribute much, if anything at all. Finally it was Joe who brought the matter to a head.

Drawing close to the old man one day, he nodded in the direction of Peter and said, "What are you paying him?"

"Paying?" snapped the old man "*Paying!* I'm not paying him anything. He's learning and I'm keeping him in rations. You don't pay a jackaroo for learning the job."

"Jackaroo," scoffed Joe. "They went out with the ark. And in any case, you're not even treating him like they used to be treated. He's entitled to meals at the house, clothing, a bit of civility on your part, and some pocket money. You're not even giving him the privileges of a rouseabout."

"Then take him," said McMichael. "I don't want him."

"I would if I could," said Joe, "but I can't offer him anything."

"In that case stop talking about him," said McMichael. "Get your shearing done and get out."

It was over a week before the road was clear enough to allow Joe to do this. On his last night Peter sat with him a long time in the rough shed.

"Please take me with you, Joe."

"I'd like to, son, but I can't."

"Let me work for you for nothing."

"It wouldn't work, son. No, you stay here. When things brighten up you can find yourself a better place, but not just at present. Keep away from McMichael as much as you can. Do what he says, and he'll keep you around. He needs you, don't worry. There will be plenty of green fodder around during the next few weeks, and you'll find a lot of interesting things happening. I may be back in a month or two if the old boy gets enough sheep in."

Joe left early next morning before Peter was up. As the sound of the old car faded in the distance, the boy turned his head into his pillow to stop the tears from running down his face.

Chapter Thirteen

HORSES DO NOT HAVE WINGS—BUT ONE FLIES

PETER WAS SURPRISED at how quickly the floods went down. The flats round the homestead gradually became visible, with perhaps some water still lying in the hollows. Soon, with the exception of the immediate river area, where the river continued to flow strongly, the country was free of water.

A large number of sheep had been caught by the water and drowned, so McMichael told the boys to go out and collect them into heaps for disposal. From a shed he extracted an old tractor, and a kind of drag. In a short time, using these, Peter and Jet had cleared the area for a kilometre or so in every direction. In due course, when enough dead sheep had been got together, McMichael had them doused with oil and the heaps set alight.

It was disgusting work, but Peter realised that the health of all at the station depended on the immediate area being cleared. Just the same, it was a relief when the old man ordered both the boys to take a day off from this, in order to go down the river to see what had happened to the horse which had been swept away.

After some hours they found its body lodged high in a tree, and debated for some time as to how they might recover the saddle which still appeared to be in good condition.

Jet was intrigued about the whole find. However, the smell drove Peter off some distance.

"You go downstream and see if there are any more dead sheep there," said Jet. "I'll meet you back here in about two hours." With that, he moved off in the direction of the homestead.

Peter returned to the spot some time later, to find Jet, with a canvas bag, standing near the tree and looking up at the horse.

"What are you going to do?"

The boy grinned and held up four sticks of gelignite. "Pinched these from old McMichael. We'll blow the ruddy tree down and then we'll be able to get the saddle."

"How? It will still be on the horse."

"Hadn't thought of that."

"What about blowing the horse up?" suggested Peter, who had never seen gelignite used. "Then we'll be able to get the saddle easier."

"Good idea," was the reply from Jet, whose

sole experience with explosives had been to watch his father and uncle blow up stumps from a distant spot, so far away that he could only guess what they were doing. However, Jet had no intention of yielding his superior place to this city kid.

He extracted a long length of fuse and cut it into four pieces. He then crimped a detonator on to each fuse with a pair of pliers he had brought, and placed one in each stick of gelignite in the same way he had seen his father do.

"Where do you think we should put them?" he asked.

Peter looked up at the dead animal. Its mouth was open giving its face a horrible leer.

"One in there," suggested Peter. Holding his breath the boy swung up into the tree and wedged a stick of explosive between the teeth of the dead animal. The fuse hung down within convenient reach.

"Another here," said Peter, taking a stick and putting it in the fork of the tree in which the horse was wedged.

"Better put in another for good measure," suggested Jet. They did so.

"We seem to have all the explosives one end," noted Peter. "I think we need a stick at the rear."

Jet tugged a strand of hair from the horse's tail and used it to tie the last of the explosive

to the rear leg of the unfortunate animal. They then both dropped to the ground and surveyed their handiwork.

"Will the fuses be long enough?" asked Peter.

"Sure," said Jet, with conviction. "You light the two at the middle and the one at the end, while I climb up and light the one in its mouth."

Both boys were completely unaware of the type of fuse they were using and, indeed, would not have known whether it was quick or slow burning. Jet's only instruction was, "When they're lit, run like blazes."

Peter waited till Jet was up the tree and had his match alight, before he struck his. He was aware all the time of the abominable smell, but had been so engrossed in his task that for a time he seemed to overlook it.

The fuse dangling from the horse's mouth was sizzling as Jet dropped to the ground. Peter lit the two middle fuses and then wasted valuable time when his match went out and he had to strike another. However, his last fuse was sizzling merrily, when he heard Jet yell, *"Run! Run! Run like hell!"* There was such urgency that he dropped his matches, swung down and ran.

Common sense should have told him to run to the nearest hollow and fling himself down, but in a panic he ran blindly, with Jet a few paces ahead of him.

They had proceeded about twenty metres when from behind them there were three most shattering and dreadful explosions, and they were both bowled over along the ground.

The air suddenly became filled with myriad pieces of putrefying horseflesh, which descended on them like meat from a mincing machine, while parts of the tree, which had also been blown off, fell with sickening thumps around them.

Shocked and horrified, the boys rose to run further, when with a terrific thump, the hind-end of the horse, which had been blown ahead of them with its fuse still attached, went off with another roar, scattering the internal contents of the horse in the boys faces so that, blinded and sickened, they ran in circles, not sure how much of the shredded flesh was theirs, and how much came from the horse.

Peter wiped the blood from his face, sure that his eyes had been blown out, and frightened to feel. Jet tried to clear his face too and, not succeeding, ran to the river, and flung himself in. Peter followed close behind and was relieved to feel the water washing away the dreadful mess which had been blown over them.

The river was not now dangerous and they were able to stand on the bottom, where they continued to wash the filthy mess from their skin and clothes.

"'Struth," said Peter, "I'll never try that again." He was rubbing mud over his face to try to get rid of the putrid smell, which seemed to be permanently attached to him.

In due course, when it appeared that no amount of water would make the situation any better, the two boys walked back to the scene of the explosion.

The tree was just a stump and, apart from pulverised flesh for scores of metres in all directions, the horse no longer existed. Of the saddle there was no sign.

"I don't think we'd better tell ol' Mac about this," said Jet. "He wouldn't like it."

They both slunk back to the station, making sure that McMichael did not notice their coming. Peter took all his clothes and soaked them in a large drum.

That night McMichael came over to leave some rations. As he came close to Peter, his nose, generally quite insensitive to such things, began to wrinkle. He looked at the boy.

"By gosh, son," he commented, "I think you need a bath. Come over to the house some time and I'll lend you a bar of soap."

Peter did not reply.

Chapter Fourteen

ESCAPE

THEIR ESCAPADE WITH the dead horse seemed to draw Jet and Peter together. Jet knew he had lost face, but this time he did not seem to mind. In fact he seemed to think the whole thing so funny that he could not refrain from referring to it, and giggling madly each time.

McMichael was attracted to the spot in the next few days by the myriad crows having a magnificent feast, and in due time Jet had to tell him what had happened. He was extremely angry, especially over the loss of the saddle, and took out his anger on Peter, driving the boy all day long and finding fault with everything he did.

Peter put up with this for some time, but one unkind remark by McMichael stung him into a terse reply which reflected on McMichael's parentage and character.

The old man gave him a punch which rolled him along the ground, his breath knocked out of him. McMichael stood over him with his heavy boots, daring him to repeat his remark.

"One more word from you, Devlin, and you go."

Peter picked himself up, and to avoid further trouble, set himself about the task McMichael had originally ordered him to do. Inwardly he was seething, but he knew there was nothing he could do about it.

Late that day the old man told him to be ready for movement early the next morning. The whole party was going out to the cattle paddocks, about twenty-five kilometres out.

Next morning Peter quickly ate an early breakfast, and went over to the loading ramp, where Jet and the two stockmen were waiting. Four horses were loaded in the big truck and then McMichael came out to drive it. The two stockmen sat in the driving cab, but the boys stood on each side of it, holding on, and at the same time keeping an eye on the horses.

The country was now becoming green after the heavy rains and the sheep they passed seemed quite content with the luxury of fresh food. Peter was surprised to notice that, as they moved further from the homestead, the country improved, and from among the stunted bushes there rose some quite large trees.

At last they came to a long range, well covered with trees, and with several deep water holes, which seemed to be spring fed. The cattle appeared to be in good condition despite the long dry season, and did not take much notice of their coming.

They spent a whole day in one area, rounding up the young cattle which had not been branded, and marking them with the station brand. Then they moved on further, and the stockmen were sent out to bring in the clean-skins.

In the course of a day they brought in many, but this time, as they were branded, McMichael told Peter and Jet to drive them back to their former camp.

"I want to build up the herd down there," he explained.

The weather was mild, and Peter enjoyed the trips, as the animals were easy to handle and there was no hurry. This continued for a week, with the camp moving further and further out and more and more beasts being brought in.

One day Peter remarked to Jet, "Old Mac ought to do well out of this. It will make up for the loss of his sheep in the flood."

"He ought to," remarked Jet. "These cost him nothing."

"What do you mean?"

"We ain't on Boolgana."

"Where are we then?"

"Next door—this is Henga Downs."

"You mean we're pinching these cattle?"

"Depends. These are clean-skins. No one can

prove who owns them. Cattle country overlaps a bit, and on the border spots, there's a bit of give and take. With Mac it's all take."

"I don't like it," said Peter, visions of cowboy pictures he had seen flashing through his mind. "What happens if we get caught?"

"Dunno—we haven't up to now."

That afternoon there came the sound of an aeroplane in the distance.

"That's the Henga Downs plane," said Jet.

At that time they were all camped in the one spot. When he heard the plane, McMichael ran to the truck and drove it under the cover of some trees. The men and the horses followed.

The plane moved round the area for some time, but did not spot them.

"We move back tonight," said McMichael. "You can start now with the horses and I'll pick you up back at the first camp."

Peter was glad when they reached their original camp.

"No one can do anything about us here," Jet informed Peter. "We're back on Mac's land. He's done pretty well out of it."

Next day they reloaded the horses, and finally arrived back at the homestead.

In that time Peter had made a decision. Somehow or other he must leave this place and, come what might, get at least as far as the main road. He had between ten and twenty dollars, counting what Joe had given him. It should be enough to take him to a town, however small.

That night he went through his gear, discarding all he would not need. He decided to keep his case and haversack, but to reduce the contents, so that the load was as light as possible. By the light of his lamp he studied the map. It would take him a day-and-a-half to get to the road. The Boolgana turnoff was forty kilometres either way down the loop road from the main highway, and when he reached this small road, he would have to decide whether to ride along it to its junction with the highway or cut across country.

He intended to ride—this was clear. He would take a horse, and release it to find its way home when he had no further need of it.

During the next few days he carefully conserved his rations, and on one or two occasions when McMichael was away, slipped into the house, took some cans of meat, and helped himself to a number of small items of food, making sure that there was no sign that he had been in the house. He felt that he was entitled to these to make up for the wages McMichael had withheld from him.

The place was as dirty as it had been when he had first entered it, some months before, and he was glad to leave it.

He noticed that Jet was watching him carefully, but dared not give the boy any inkling of his plans. That Jet suspected something was clear when he returned unexpectedly to his quarters and found Jet looking into his suitcase.

For a moment he misunderstood what he was doing.

"What do you want? You've no right to open my things."

Jet was not upset. He turned slowly.

"You're nicking," he said, more as a statement of fact than a question.

"What I'm doing is my own business. Now get out."

"I wasn't going to pinch anything."

"Who said you were? I trust you."

Jet walked outside without any further comment.

Peter had lost all count of time and did not even know what day it was. If he had known, he would have tried to leave the station at a time when he would have been able to pick up the weekly mail-truck, which left stores and provisions at the station turnoff.

McMichael was so irregular in his journeys, either to bring in the mail or to collect the stores, that this was no indication of which week it was.

In all the time he had been at the station,

Peter had received no letters, and though he had expected that Mrs Sloan or Ian might have written, he was not really surprised when they did not. He had written once to Mrs Sloan, and had asked McMichael to post it for him. The old man had merely grunted and put the letter in his pocket.

It was useless therefore to plan his departure for any particular time, for one day was as good as another. The main thing was for him to leave when the heat was out of the atmosphere. In this he was fortunate, for the hot summer now seemed to be passing away and the more agreeable autumn was well under way.

Nevertheless he still found it difficult to make the final decision. It was finally forced on him. McMichael had decided to do some repairs on one of the trucks. He had the two boys assisting him. Peter was either too slow handing him a spanner, or did not hear, for suddenly the man became very irritable, and when Peter did stoop down to pick up the right tool, in a sudden rage the man flung the entire tool-kit at the boy.

Peter stepped adroitly aside, and the tools scattered in the dust in all directions. This so enraged the man further, that he made a move towards the boy, as if to strike or kick him. Peter did not stay, but went away to a safe distance.

Still bellowing with rage, and unable to vent his spleen on the boy physically, McMichael went roaring over to the boy's room. From a distance Peter watched him throw all his possessions out of the door—his case, his haversack, and even the bed.

Still raging, the man went back to his own house. When it was safe enough the boy moved in and, picking up his scattered possessions, took them and began to move towards the river.

He was not quite ready to leave the place, as for the sake of safety he had hidden his food supply under the shearers' kitchen. He would have to wait till dark before daring to venture back. Jet watched him go without a word.

Peter spent a day in the shade of some white gums on the way to the river, keeping a wary eye towards the station in case McMichael should come after him, but in all that time he did not see a living soul move anywhere, either round the station or between it and the river.

When it was dusk, after hiding his gear carefully, he began to make his way back. He had emptied his haversack so that he could fill it with food. As he neared the buildings, he saw a dark form. It was Jet.

"I was coming down to see what you were doing," he said.

"I'm going to get some food I stowed away. Then I'm going to pinch a horse."

"You wouldn't get away with it," commented Jet. "Ol' Mac would hear you. Leave it to me. I know how to do it quietly."

"Okay. I'll go back for the food and you get the horse. Thanks."

Peter crept through the yard. Fortunately the dogs knew him and did not bark. He was able to find all his food, as well as a large water-bottle. He filled this at the tank, and then stowed everything in his haversack.

With due care he moved back towards the river. About half a kilometre down the track he found Jet. He was holding two horses.

"Why two? I don't want a pack animal." The moon was just rising. In its light, Peter saw that Jet was carrying a sack.

"I'm coming too."

"You're not!"

"Yes, I am. My pa told me to."

"You told your pa?"

"Of course. He's a good bloke. Reckons you need someone to look after you."

Peter was taken aback. "It will cause trouble."

Jet laughed. "For who? Ol' Mac says a thing to my pa or Tom, and he has nobody. Nobody at all."

"How far are you coming?"

"Dunno. Depends on how far you go."

Peter stood irresolute for a moment. Then

suddenly his feeling of loneliness and hopelessness vanished.

"Come on, Jet fellow. We'll go off and get rich together."

"Dunno about that, but it would have been mighty lonely at Boolgana after you went."

There was no need for further words. A few minutes of careful riding and they were at the gum trees. Peter retrieved all his things. Jet handed him another sack.

"Throw your case away. Put all your stuff in here. It will be easier riding than lugging that case."

Peter did so and hurled the case away. "What's keeping us?" he asked. "Off we go."

"You go on," said Jet. "I have something personal I want to attend to."

Peter kept his horse moving slowly onward, while Jet circled round and disappeared in the direction of the station.

Peter had proceeded a short distance, when he was suddenly struck by the thought that Jet was perhaps going to do something silly such as setting alight to the place. He quickly turned his horse and followed the other boy.

By now the moon had risen fully, and the station was lit with a silvery light. There was no sound or movement. Suddenly Peter heard the tractor being started up. He saw it emerge from its shed and watched in astonishment as,

with a slim form holding the wheel, it made a direct line for the side of the homestead.

A second before it struck, the dark form jumped off and disappeared behind the tractor shed. There was a terrific crash as the tractor hit the house, and without stopping went right through the wall and disappeared. At the same moment Jet came riding furiously back, and Peter, realising that there was nothing he could do, turned his horse and went full-pelt after him.

It was as well that he did so. From behind came the screaming yells of McMichael and a fusillade of shots in their direction. Peter crouched low and raced away.

Two kilometres away, the boys pulled up together.

"You fool," yelled Peter, "now you'll really have McMichael after us."

"Not for a couple of days. It will take all of that before my pa finds the missing distributor caps off the trucks—and I let the horses out. My pa and Tom won't be able to catch one in three days."

"Your dad's better than that."

"Of course he is, when he wants to be."

Peter gave up. Jet had thought of everything.

That night they travelled twelve kilometres along the river. Then they set up camp. They were up at dawn, but did not stay to eat breakfast, fearful that by some chance McMichael might have caught a horse himself, and would be on them before they knew it. They stopped for some food later in the morning.

All that day they travelled, moving steadily but not too fast, and covered a further fifty or more kilometres. In midmorning of the next day they came out on the road.

They did so cautiously, making sure that, neither at the river-crossing nor between it and the station turnoff, was there anyone lurking to ambush them.

"What do we do now?" asked Peter. "Turn up the road and follow it to the highway or cut across country?"

"Cross-country would be safer," said Jet. "We can keep with the river most of the way."

Struck by a sudden thought, Peter said, "You remain here, Jet. I'll ride to the mail-bin, just in case there is a letter for me." He moved up the road.

There was a large quantity of mail. In the back of the drum, Peter found a number of letters addressed to himself and, in two uncollected bundles, several more. It was apparent that McMichael, though not unscrupulous enough to destroy Peter's mail, had nevertheless thrown it back into the mail container.

Peter stuffed the letters down his shirt, while he debated whether to leave a last note for the old man. He began to think of some apt phrases he could put in it, but in the end changed his mind, and instead took the stub of a pencil from his pocket and wrote on the back of one of the bills addressed to the man:

You'll get your horses back. We've just borrowed them. Take the hire charges out of my wages.

P. Devlin.

With a last look round, he moved back to the river where Jet had prepared a meal. While he ate Peter looked through his mail.

There were several letters from Mrs Sloan, asking about his progress and worrying a little because she had not heard from him. There were some letters from Ian, slipped in, telling him about school. It seemed an echo from another world.

In the last letter Mrs Sloan had enclosed five dollars, and when he turned to the second page, he found she had added a postscript after completing the letter.

Peter dear, I have wonderful news. The Red Cross report that your father has been listed alive and well as a prisoner of war.

Peter dropped the letter, his hands shaking and his face losing all its colour.

Jet noticed. "What's the matter?" he asked.

"I've just heard that my father is alive in a prisoner of war camp in Hanoi."

"Good," said Jet, "but it won't help you none now."

It was not said in a manner meant to offend, but rather to bring him to a sense of the reality of his present position.

Peter nodded. "You always were pretty direct, Jet, but I understand. Just the same, it makes me feel better."

"Me too. I don't hold with people getting killed."

All tension gone, Peter burst out laughing. "You're neat, Jet. I agree with you."

"What else you got there?" asked Jet, pointing to the rest of the letters.

There was one without a stamp. Peter tore it open. It was from Joe.

I rite this befor I go on. here is some mony. I would have took you but it aint any life for a boy. go to daniel creek. I have writ to jack williams. jack is a good bloke he will help you.

your freind Joe

Attached were two ten-dollar bills.

Peter read the note aloud to Jet.

"He's mighty," said Jet. "I wish he'd have took me along."

"He's mighty to me too," said Peter, "and always will be."

"How long do we stay here?" asked Jet, getting impatient. "The sooner we get to the main road the better. McMichael will be after us soon."

They packed up their gear and began to move across country.

Chapter Fifteen

FORTUNE SHINES

PETER AND JET ARRIVED at the highway that afternoon. As soon as they came in sight of it, they took their gear from the horses and dismounted. They then drove the horses away, and saw them galloping back towards the station where, no doubt, they would arrive a few days later.

All else failing, Peter had decided that he would stop one of the overland buses and pay the fare of Jet and himself, for as far as the money he had would take them. He still had the tattered map, and already had learnt that if they intended to seek out Joe's friend, Jack Williams, at Daniel Creek, they still had a fairly long distance to go on the highway before they turned off some 200 kilometres further inland.

Peter had studied the legend on the map closely. MINING AND PASTORAL it said. Daniel Creek might be anything these days—a declining town, a sleepy hollow used as a centre for the district, or a boom town, with wealth from mining and the pastoral industry. The map did not tell them.

The boys sat on the side of the road. There was a moderate flow of traffic, but for the time most of it seemed to be going the wrong way.

Peter did not know much about the art of hitch-hiking, but Jet did, and soon had by sheer impudence forced a large semi-trailer to pull to a halt.

The driver was quite good-humoured about it. "Climb into the van," he invited. "The side door's open. There's plenty of room. I dropped a load a short distance back. Where do you want to go?"

"Drop us off at the Daniel Creek road junction please," said Peter.

They climbed into the huge van. The driver revved the diesel engine up and the truck was travelling again.

The great compartment was only half full of crates, and in the area near the door there was a large space. Some of it was already occupied. An Aboriginal family occupied a corner, a couple of hippy-type young men with long hair and print trousers sat in another, while full length across the other door a large fellow smelling of whisky lay on his back, sound asleep and snoring loudly.

Despite its size, the powerful transport roared

along at a steady eighty kilometres an hour, and Peter, exhausted from the events of the last few days, dropped off to sleep. He was quite comfortable, for thick canvas covers lay on the floor.

Several times the vehicle stopped, and Jet peered out to see the reason. Once it was for fuel, and so he wakened Peter and they rushed into the roadhouse and bought some food.

To Peter it was unreal to be drinking cans of iced coke and munching hamburgers, even if the coke did cost forty-five cents a can and the hamburgers a dollar each. It was all cheap enough, when one had been denied these luxuries for so long and had, in fact, forgotten that they existed.

At the next stop the hippies slipped out, and on the third the Aboriginal family. The drunk still snored loudly, and soon Peter and Jet dropped off to sleep too.

They awoke some hours later. It was dark, and the vehicle was grinding to a halt. A flash of light showed that they were again at a roadhouse.

The driver came down along the huge van calling out, "This is as far as you go with me, kids. Hop off!"

The boys grabbed their belongings and jumped down. Peter fumbled in his pocket and handed the driver a dollar. He laughed.

"You'll need it more than me, kid. Thanks just the same," and stuck it back in Peter's pocket.

"You're a sport, mate," said Jet.

They moved off down towards the roadhouse. It was a hive of activity, with vehicles coming and going, and from the huge restaurant there came the delicious smell of food. A little further away, a well-lit building had a sign on it SHOWERS.

"Come on," said Peter. "We'll have a good wash and then have some tea."

"Who's paying?" asked Jet. "You need to be a millionaire to eat in these places."

"It's okay. I've still got a bit put by, and considering everything we've been through, we deserve a good feed now."

Together they moved over to the showers and, putting their gear in a place where they could keep an eye on it, they had soon stripped and were revelling in the delight of the hot water.

"This is the life for me," yelled Peter.

"A bit too posh for me," yelled back Jet, "but it'll do."

They each pulled a clean shirt out of their sacks, and Peter found a mirror and combed his hair. It was getting longer than he liked, and had not had a pair of scissors near it since Joe had cut it for him many weeks before with his wool shears. It combed into shape quite well, however.

Peter handed Jet the comb, and the boy also combed his hair right back. They made a handsome pair of boys.

In the restaurant they tarried so long over what they would have that the waitress began to get fidgety, and as a hint said, "I'll come back."

Eventually they settled on T-bone steak, bacon, and four eggs each.

"You hungry or something?" asked the girl.

"You watch when you bring it," said Peter, "and snatch your hand away fast."

"Quite a funny boy, aren't you?" she responded. "And what will you have for afters?"

"Fruit salad and ice cream," said Peter.

"Me too," echoed Jet.

Eating the meal, Peter found it hard to believe that less than a week before they had both been living at Boolgana, now hundreds of kilometres away. Here indeed was life. He determined that Jet and he would enjoy every minute of it until their money ran out.

"Golly," said Jet, "a man don't eat like this every day."

"Some do," said Peter, finishing off the last of the bread and washing it down with his third cup of coffee.

They were reluctant to move away from the

table, but with their hunger satisfied, there was no sense in staying any longer.

Peter managed to attract the attention of one of the petrol station attendants once they were outside.

"What's the chance of a lift to Daniel Creek from here?" he asked him.

"At night, nil. There's too much wild life on the road, as well as stray sheep and cattle. Hang round till morning and you'll get a lift. Plenty of heavy vehicles are going through all the time. It's about two hundred kilometres."

The boys began to move off. The man followed them.

"Why don't you bed down over there," he suggested, pointing to a grassy area to the rear of the roadhouse. "The boss won't mind as long as you don't try to steal his fowls."

They did so. Peter put his trusty sack on the ground and made a pillow out of his haversack. Jet just curled up on the grass and fell asleep immediately. They both felt at peace with the world.

Chapter Sixteen

ALL THANKS TO JOE

THE BOYS SLEPT WELL but woke early. They had a shower, and after Peter had counted his money, went in to the restaurant for an early breakfast.

They had just finished eating when the attendant, who had just come on duty, poked his head round the door.

"I've arranged for a ride for you blokes," he said. "Come on."

After being kicked around for so long, Peter was astonished to find that there were still people who were thoughtful and decent.

"That's pretty nice of you," he told the man. "We didn't expect that."

"You're in the north now, son. Most people round these parts are pretty co-operative."

Their transport was an open truck piled with provisions and goods covered by large tarpaulins.

"If you find yourselves a possie right behind the cab," the driver told them, "you won't get too much of the dust. It won't be too hot today, and we stop quite regularly."

"We don't mind," said Peter. "It's good of you to take us."

"I pass through Daniel Creek about midday and so you won't be there long. Anyway it's a scenic trip, if you like scenery. There isn't anything else like it in these parts."

In due course the vehicle took off. The boys each had a well-filled water-bottle, and Peter had bought extra food.

For several kilometres the road was tarred, but later this dropped behind, as they passed over long stretches of dirt road, in various stages of construction and in every condition from good to bad.

The truck bumped and swayed, and it was impossible to see anything behind it through the great swirling clouds of red dust. However, the boys were able to watch the countryside ahead, as gradually the red plains disappeared and they rode through an extensive range of hills which rose high on either side.

The hills were green on their slopes, but suddenly rose into rugged, rocky cliffs which, with their varied colours and formations, impressed Peter very much. In one area he could see varied colours including deep purples, and his mind went back to the years before, when on the walls of the lounge of his home in the city he had seen a splendid print of almost the same sort of country.

"See," he said, pointing it out to Jet, "it looks like a Namatjira picture."

"Who?" asked Jet.

"One of your mob—the great Aboriginal painter."

"Never heard of him," said Jet. "Only blokes I know in that line paint houses."

"Well, he was pretty good."

"Was? Is he dead?"

"Yes—not too nice a story. His pictures are priceless, but I don't think they did him any good."

"Nothing does us any good," said Jet, "but it don't worry me."

Peter did not reply. His own position wasn't very good, but what the future held for Jet was another matter. It wasn't much good thinking of a distant future, however, when he was not sure what the day would provide.

They were going to some remote town at the suggestion of a kindly, illiterate shearer. Who Jack Williams was, and whether he would want them, they had no idea.

During one of the stops Peter asked the driver.

"Jack Williams? He's the local pub-keeper. Good bloke. You know him?"

"No, but a friend told us to contact him."

"You couldn't do better."

Much heartened, the boys climbed back on to the truck and waited impatiently for the journey to end. The road took them through range after range of fine country. Many signs along the road indicated the turnoffs to stations, and at intervals they saw large flocks of sheep and many cattle. The summer rains had apparently fallen heavily, as the entire country was covered with grass and undergrowth.

A few kilometres out of Daniel Creek, the asphalt began again. Knowing that the importance of a town could generally be guessed by the length of tarred road in and out of it, Peter realised that this might not be as small a place as he had imagined.

Soon they crossed a railway line, and within minutes the road was leading down between irregularly spaced but well-built stone houses, each with a plot of grass in front of it, and surrounded by its own clump of trees.

The truck began to slow down as it came into the beginning of the town. They passed green parks and gardens, and came to a large community shopping-centre. Here the driver pulled up.

"Get out here," he called. "Jack Williams' pub is in the next street. You can't miss it."

They threw their gear down on to the footpath, and before they could thank the driver, he had moved off.

After months of loneliness, Peter was quite amazed to see the evidence of so many people—rows of parked cars, women wheeling prams down the shady verandahs of the shops, a group of toddlers playing in a kindergarten, and, most astonishingly of all, a large fountain gushing water in all directions. They moved along the footpath and found a milk bar. To Peter it was almost as though he had been transported to some magical place.

Surely Boolgana Downs never existed. Surely Josh McMichael was a figment of his imagination. Surely all that had happened since he had left the city had been a mad dream.

After downing a couple of milk shakes each, they found a toilet where they washed themselves. Peter changed his shirt and also took off his rough jeans, putting on a pair of grey flannel trousers. Jet, who was uneasy about it all, contented himself with combing his hair and brushing the dust off his clothes. Peter had been wearing boots, but he found a pair of shoes in his sack and put them on—the first time for many months.

Jet was barefooted, but this did not seem out of place.

"Now to find Mr Williams," said Peter. "I don't know what he can do for us, but we'd better try him."

They were both shocked when, on walking

along to the next street, they saw the hotel. It was a huge modern structure, with shaded beer gardens, big gleaming doors to saloons, and it towered three storeys high. To one side there were motel units, surrounded by grass and gardens, and around it all vast car parks filled with cars. Both the boys were awed. Surely a man who controlled such opulence would not be troubled with their worries.

Peter's resolution failed him. He had been picturing in his mind a small country hotel, with the owner sunning himself outside while waiting for custom, but this was something comparable with the huge hotels he had seen in the city.

At last the boys summoned up enough courage to make at least an effort to find Mr Williams. Together they walked round the building. They peered into the bars and saloons, but knew that in none of these, even if they saw the man, would they be able to explain their purpose.

Finally they came to a section where a large sign said OFFICE.

Jet refused to come in, and so Peter pushed the glass door open and moved into the air-conditioned coolness of a long corridor. At the end there was a window. He moved up to it and found himself at a counter with a large office behind it.

A shapely blonde was standing by a window,

languidly filing her finger-nails. She saw the boy, but made no indication that she had done so. A phone rang, and she moved over to the switchboard to reply to it. She had false eyelashes and wore a golden wig. Peter judged her to be not more than a few years older than he was. The girl concluded the telephone conversation, and then opened an account book on her desk, which was beside the switchboard.

When after a few minutes it was apparent that she was not going to attend to him, Peter pressed the bell on the counter. The girl moved over to the counter.

"There's no need to do that. I'll get round to you in due course." She moved back to her desk and did some figuring and then, when Peter had almost given up any hope of communication with her, she asked, "And what can I do for you, boy?"

Peter blushed, but kept his temper.

"I want to see Mr Williams."

"You do? Have you an appointment?"

"No. But I think he expects me."

"Does he? Then sit over there and wait."

Peter moved obediently over to a long padded seat. The girl took her time. He heard her ask for Mr Williams, and waited expectantly. The phone rang, and the switchboard continued to demand her attention. After fifteen minutes Peter walked over to the counter.

She ignored him. Then after a few minutes she said quite casually, "Mr Williams is out."

"When will he be in?"

"Don't ask me."

"But I am."

"Don't be cheeky, boy. Now go away."

Peter walked outside to Jet. "No luck. Mr Williams is out. What do we do next?"

"Wait," said Jet, who was used to waiting.

They stayed at the hotel all the afternoon. It was an anticlimax after coming so far, but Peter realised that he should never have set too great hopes on what might happen when they got to Daniel Creek.

Once or twice during the afternoon he presented himself at the desk. Each time the beautiful girl, when she deigned to recognise his presence, shook her head, but gave him no more information.

It was clear to both boys that they would not be allowed to camp in the town, and that soon they would have to move to the outskirts, at least, to sleep.

Somewhat dejectedly Peter was beginning to put their things together, when he decided to have one last try to contact the hotel owner. He was surprised to find that the receptionist who had treated him so disdainfully had gone, and in her place was an older woman. She attended to the boy at once.

"You looking for Jack? Oh, he's around somewhere. I'll get him for you."

This was so surprising that Peter looked startled.

"Anything wrong?" asked the woman.

"No, but I've been trying to get him all day and the other one said he was out."

"Lazy little devil," said the woman. "He was only out getting the mail for a short time."

She took up a microphone and began paging for Jack Williams.

Soon a door opened at the end of the corridor, and the largest man Peter had ever seen came through the door. He was not fat, but he was of such massive frame and height that the boy stood staring at him until the man called out, "You wouldn't be young Devlin, would you?"

"Yes, sir. I am."

"You got Joe's message and followed his advice, I see."

"No, sir. I ran away and I only got his message afterwards."

"Joe must think a lot of you, son. I knew him during the war. He wrote to me and even put a phone call through to me about you."

"That was Joe, sir. He's a wonderful fellow. I hope I'm not putting you out."

"No, son, not at all," was the good-natured reply. "Seems you had a bad time with old McMichael. I've heard of him, even this far away. You lost your dad in Vietnam, I believe."

"Yes, sir, but I heard the other day that he is now a prisoner of war."

"What about your mother?"

"She left me. I don't know where she is."

"You certainly copped it, son. Never mind, I'll find something for you. Have you got any luggage?"

"A haversack, and a few things in a sack."

"Go and get them. I'll put you up here while I sort out something for you—turn you over to the wife to look after."

Peter hung back. "It's pretty kind of you sir, but I have Jet."

"Jet?"

"Yes sir, Jet Mercedes Benz."

"Oh. One of them."

"No, sir, not one of them. Jet has been very loyal to me. He saved my life once, and when I left, he left too."

"How old is he?"

"Younger than me—about fourteen."

Williams scratched his head. Then he smiled.

"I can see it's a case of take one, take both. You're pretty loyal to him too, aren't you, sonny?"

"He's my friend."

"Okay. He won't provide much trouble—probably much more handy round these parts than you. I'll take a chance on both of you. I'm very fond of old Joe and I'd like to do him a good turn. You seem a decent enough kid."

Williams went to the desk. He wrote on a piece of hotel stationery.

"Take this," he said. "Over behind the motel is the old building. We use it for staff quarters. We've a few spare rooms there. You can take up your quarters there until I can find you something definite. In the meantime you can both help round the place. We'll discuss wages later. Give this note to Mrs Watson over there. She'll show you round and arrange for your meals. Want any cash in advance?"

"No thank you, sir. Joe left twenty dollars for my fare up here and we've some of that left."

"Right. You're fixed for the time being."

"You're pretty decent, Mr Williams."

The man laughed. "Rubbish. If Joe thinks you're all right, it's okay with me. He's a pretty good judge is old Joe."

Peter could not get back to Jet fast enough.

"Jet boy, we're made! We've both got jobs and lodgings. Come on before this note in my hand suddenly dissolves and I know it's just another dream."

"How did you do it?"

"I didn't. It was dear old Joe. Mr Williams thinks a lot of him and he wanted to help me."

"What about me? Joe didn't mention me. How come I'm included?"

"That was easy. Mr Williams said you'd probably do a better job round these parts than me."

"That's what I told you a long time ago," said Jet with a pleased smirk on his face. "I'm a man and you're still a boy."

Chapter Seventeen

ALL'S RIGHT WITH THE WORLD

PETER WAS STILL TOO YOUNG to know that life has its ups and downs—that its bitter moments are sooner or later followed by sweet ones; but he was learning fast.

The transition from life at Boolgana to life at Daniel Creek seemed to him to be almost beyond belief. Even Jet responded to the new circumstances and, when after the first week they received wages, he brought himself some shoes and a pair of slacks. Peter realised that Jet's city upbringing had not been entirely forgotten. It was apparent that Jet, now that he was away from the influence of his father and uncle, wished once again to be part of the modern community he had once known.

As far as Peter had found out, Jet had been fostered by a well-meaning city woman till the age of eleven. She had died suddenly, and his father, learning of this, had made successful claim to him. Peter was aware that Jet's rejection of this previous life had been forced on him by his circumstances, but he wondered if he was doing the right thing now in tearing the boy away from his relatives, and a situation to which he had appeared to be adapted and reconciled.

As to his own future, Peter could not see beyond the next day, and indeed he did not wish to do so. Jack Williams appeared well satisfied with their work at the place. When Peter received his first week's pay, he was staggered to have so much money all at once.

He did not know it, but Williams had also not been idle. The radio-telephone to the city had been busy on a number of nights, while the man tried to piece together the circumstances which had driven Peter from the city. He had been in touch with the headmaster of the boy's school, and there had been a debate as to whether Peter should be returned there to complete his education.

A number of Peter's friends had been located, including Mrs Sloan, who had not yet received Peter's first letter telling of his experiences during the past months.

Armed with all this, Williams called Peter to his office one evening. He was pleased to see the change in the boy, and to notice that there was already an air of confidence in his manner.

"I've got a decision to make about you, son," Mr Williams began.

"You're not dissatisfied with Jet and me, sir?"

"Far from it, laddie, but you can't go on like this."

"I could. It's much better than before."

"Yes, I know all that, but then you thought things a little hopeless. You believed your dad to be dead and there was no one who cared about you."

"There were people who did. I had a lot of friends."

"Yes, I know. I have spoken to them."

Peter looked surprised.

"Yes, son. I've made a few enquiries about you and they have confirmed my opinion that you mustn't just be allowed to drift around as you are. It may be a long time yet, but one day your dad is going to return. He won't want to find his kid has been neglected."

"I can look after myself till that happens."

"Maybe, but you've got your education to consider too."

"I'm afraid I'll have to forget about that."

"No, not necessarily. Would you like to go back to school?"

"Sir, I just couldn't. It would seem kid-stuff after the last six months or so. I want to continue my studies, but if I could do so and work as well, I would feel happier."

"Do you want to go back to the city?"

"No, Mr Williams. Somehow or other, this

country has got under my skin and I like it. Then there's Jet."

"Blow Jet," said Williams. "We can always fix up something for him."

Peter rose. "I stick with Jet, Mr Williams. He didn't have much, but he gave it all up for me. If we could find work together on one of the stations, where things are a bit better than Boolgana Downs, I reckon it would be a great life."

"Sit down and keep your hair on, boy," said Williams with good humour. "You two certainly seem to be attached to each other. I suppose he's entitled to a break too. Leave it to me. I'll see what I can do."

So they left it at that. Both boys helped with a will round the vast establishment, doing anything required of them, both inside the buildings and in the grounds. The hours were long, but the pay was good, and it seemed as if they could go on like this forever.

By degrees they took part in the social life of the town. Jet scored best in the Police Boys' Club, where he proved no mean opponent in the boxing ring, and won a small trophy at a weekend event.

As the cool weather was coming on, the boys also put their names down for the football team. Peter was good, but even in the training sessions it was apparent that Jet was outstanding. In the first scratch match, the club officials were astonished at his natural aptitude. In the grandstand, Jack Williams was sitting next to his close friend, Harry Stewart, who had come to town for the day.

"Good heavens, Jack, where did you pick up that kid? I haven't noticed him before."

"No. He's a blow-in. Used to work with McMichael at Boolgana Downs, but I gather he made it too tough for the kid and his mate—a rather nice kid named Devlin. There he is over there, playing fullback."

"Not a bad pair. Pity we couldn't keep them round here."

"You could, Harry. I've got them working round my place, but it's not the life for two kids—and they're pretty good material, both of them."

"Brings back my younger days, Jack. I did pretty well out of the game before I came up here after the war."

"I'll say you did, you old war-horse. Collected every medal in the state and three interstate. Bet if the Japs hadn't put that hole in your leg, you'd still be playing."

"I'll say I would." He appeared to be thinking. "I could find a place for two willing lads out at Yullamooloo." He gazed slyly at his friend. "I suppose you'd be bothering me every weekend to have them back in your team."

"Why not? You can afford to let them come in each week."

"Done," said Stewart. "Let's have the kids up here after the match, and see what they think."

"Devlin's got some ideas about going on with his studies," said Williams.

"He'll have plenty of time. I work my blokes hard, but I play fair with them, Jack. You know that. They'd learn plenty at Yullamooloo. Devlin might be managerial material. You never know. Get 'em young, Jack, and train 'em right."

"That's settled then?"

"Of course."

The match ended. Jack Williams sent one of the reserves who was still loitering in the stand to bring Peter and Jet up to him, when they had showered and changed.

The boys came up eventually, well-scrubbed and both neat, in sports shirts and slacks. Jet was very carefully patterning himself on Peter.

"Well," said Jack Williams, "you play a good game—both of you. Meet a friend, Harry Stewart."

"Harry Stewart!" said Jet. "I know you. You used to be a footballer. I had your picture in my footy scrapbook when I was a kid."

"You used to be among the greats, didn't you, Mr Stewart?" put in Peter. "They even named a grandstand after you, back in the city."

"Such is fame," grinned Stewart, "even after these years. I must say you fellows don't play a bad game either."

"Thanks, Mr Stewart. It's been great meeting you. We'd better go now; we've got a bit to do for Mr Williams here."

"No hurry," said Williams. "Mr Stewart wants to ask you a question."

"Ask away," said Jet. "We've got no secrets."

"Well," said Stewart, "I'll ask you straight. How would you like to come and work for me at Yullamooloo?"

"*What?*" in tones of incredulous surprise from both boys.

They both looked at Williams. He was grinning.

"It's okay by me, boys. I made the suggestion."

"You did?"

"Yes. On one condition."

"Sir?"

"That Harry allows you weekends off to play in our footy team. You're good material. In a year or two you'll make the Senior Grade and you'll really be in."

"Work at Yullamooloo!" said Peter, pinching himself. "But, Mr Williams, that's the mightiest place in the country."

"Flattery will get you nowhere," said Stewart,

grinning with enjoyment, "but I must admit Yullamooloo's not a bad place."

"The understatement of the age," said Williams. "Okay, fellows, off you go. You're still working for me, remember! Mr Stewart can have you in a week's time, after we've kitted you out. Now off with you."

The boys tumbled down the steps of the grandstand in their excitement, and disappeared from view.

"I don't think you've done a wrong thing, Harry," said Jack Williams.

"I'm certain I haven't. Let's go and get a drink."

Peter and Jet floated out of the football ground; they floated along the road; they floated into their quarters and then, the sudden realisation of their good fortune striking them, they danced round the room, crying out, *"We're made! We're made!"*

They were—but that is another story.